Supreme Happiness

Supreme Happiness

Nelson L. Price

Broadman Press
Nashville, Tennessee

Dewey Decimal Classification: 226.93

Subject heading: BEATITUDES

Library of Congress Catalog Card Number: 78–67000

Printed in the United States of America

Foreword

When Nelson Price speaks, I listen. When he writes, I tune in right here. As the young set puts it, "This cat is together." Up-to-date as our next heartbeat; old-fashioned as the gospel; master at illustration; super relator. That's Nelson.

If he weren't doing such a superb job as a pastor, he could make a mint with some New York public relations firm.

The Beatitudes have long been favorite reading of the Christian community. They have been and always will be favorites for seekers after truth. Taking each of these famous phrases, Nelson leads us through biblical meaning into application of our daily lives.

Every one of us wants to be among "blessed are they." We all want happiness. But sometimes what we think will make us "blessed" brings only misery.

I hope this book realizes a wide audience. It can do much for the joyful to bring more joy, and for the down it can be a real lifter.

CHARLIE SHEDD

Contents

1
How to Avoid an Emotional Overdraft

It was a mild midsummer eve as we began our climb up the history-marked slopes of Kennesaw Mountain. Our family had been joined by a family of five. The children played along the way and thus avoided fatigue. One of the little girls found a cute green frog on the way up. It became her pet. By the time we reached the summit, it was well after dark. The night was still and black. Much to our delight, the Lockheed Astronomy Club was having a meeting on the rounded peak. Telescopes, large and small, were all over the place. Generous space buffs kept us busy switching from one scope to another to see what extraterrestrial treasure they had in focus. The sky was brilliant. Beauties beyond the range of one's natural eye emerged through every lens. Imaginations were ignited by what was seen.

As I looked excitedly at Saturn and her nine moons, suddenly I heard a distressed little voice crying, "I lost my frog! Where is my frog?" That slithery little creature had successfully escaped. There amid the open windows of the awesome beauty of the universe, a lowly frog had become the center of concern. The frontiers of space were forgotten for a frog. A childish preoccupation had caused the panorama of the heavens to be neglected.

That juvenile's judgment is typical of many persons' misplaced values. An absorption with absurdity had caused the stunning stellar scenes to be missed. Those who set their affection on things above can be divinely happy. Those who establish earthly things as their primary concern may thereby seek happiness, but they will only find their fantasy frog gone.

Which will it be, unlimited frontiers or uncontrollable frogs? That choice is ours. Such a choice dictates the consequence. You can choose to be divinely happy.

Poor in Spirit

Poor (ptōchos) means a beggar who lives off the alms of another person, one who humbly crouches in the presence of a superior. There is in the Greek meaning no moral or religious glorification of material poverty.

The Aramaic word behind the gospel word translated *blessed* is an exclamation meaning, "O the blessedness of . . ." The blessedness of the poor? The paupers and beggars, those who are absolutely destitute? The context is a spiritual one. The mental image evoked depicts a spiritual condition. It does not hint at physical poverty as being a virtue. It is a reference to a mental attitude. The poor in the Bible era were often thought of as being synonymous with the saintly.

Only when a person realizes himself to be spiritually bankrupt can he obtain divine happiness. It is not an innate quality of life. Neither is it an object to be sought or bought. By himself, no one can attain and maintain it. An awareness of spiritual poverty can result in spiritual prosperity.

As long as one maintains an air of independence, resulting in simulated self-sufficiency, there is no likelihood of happiness. A person, like a building, must be braced and supported from within; else, like a building without proper support, he crumbles to the ground.

In our community a group of persons leased the basement floor of a building to develop it as a beauty salon. For weeks renovation activity was underway. In spite of much work, no progress was evidenced.

Across the four-lane street was a bank. The developers were actually spending their nights tunneling under the street into the bank's vault. Upon their entering the vault, various alarms sounded. Official and police inspections of the bank found the door to the vault secure and all other things in place. They assumed there to be a malfunction in the alarm system and never thought to open the vault in consideration of someone being inside. All through the weekend the thieves worked calmly and confidently without being disturbed. The valuable contents of safe-deposit boxes were stolen.

Outside everything looked good. There were some alarming signs, but everything gave a good appearance until the bank opened on Monday and the contents of the vault were checked. An internal inspection found emptiness.

To be poor in spirit is no disgrace. It is not even a distinction. Not to acknowledge it is to suffer greater loss. Without proper internal inspection, additional loss is inevitable.

Watch for the alarm signs of pride, arrogance, brassiness, impudence, cockiness, and flashes of ego. These and other related signs indicate that something is wrong inside. Not to admit poverty of spirit is self-deception. It is a leaky decoy.

Happiness must always work from within. It is not dependent on circumstances. It is reliant on the attitude summed up in the word *poor*. It is abject poverty of spirit, resulting in relying on Christ's resources. That is the starting point. This happiness is superior to circumstances. It is an internal condition, not contingent upon externals.

One must realize that there is no personal life-supporting sufficiency within oneself. At this point there must be an acknowledged willingness to bank on Christ's account. Dividends can then be accrued.

The poor in spirit know they are dependent on God. To know one's helplessness is one thing. To acknowledge it and look for help in the right place is another.

Poverty's Pertinence

To be poor in spirit does not mean to be poor-spirited. It does not refer to a dejected, self-pitying person without backbone or "stuffin.' "

The poor in spirit are not to be confused with those who are poor in worldly circumstances. They are not the trite in spirit or the spiritually poor.

To be poor in spirit involves humility, contentment, submission, and gratitude.

There are those who are convicted of their spiritual poverty. They not only realize it—they declare it to the King.

Spiritual poverty is the beginning of spiritual nobility.

The poor in spirit do not boast of talents or attainments. They know they do not have anything they have not received from God. Job observed centuries ago, "The Lord gave and the Lord hath taken away." We need to conclude with him, "Blessed be the name of the Lord" (Job 1:21).

The poor in spirit consider themselves stewards rather than collectors in their own private wars of greed.

King David noted a balanced view of life's goods: "All things come from Thee, and of Thine own we give Thee."

To be poor in spirit is not a relative thing—it is a relevant thing. We are not to compare ourselves with others. When we do so, we grade on a curve and always come out better than we deserve. We are extraordinarily adept at picking things to relate to that make us look our best. A cat is big compared to a mouse. A cat is small in comparison to an elephant. Most of us cats pick mice for comparisons.

This fact caused Will Rogers to comment, "I always like to hear a man talk about himself because then I never hear anything but good."

Some tactful possessors of pride seek to share the glory of God. The little word *but* often inserted in their assertions is a telltale symptom of this syndrome. Some years ago, Charles E. Hughes was chief justice of the United States Supreme Court. He served as our nation's delegate to the Pan-American Conference at Havana. There an interpreter was busily whispering the flowery introduction by a local orator. Mr. Hughes stopped the aide and gave the following instruction: "Don't bother about interpreting anything until he says 'but.' Give me everything after that." We too should give God everything before and after our *buts*.

To be poor in spirit is relevant; that is, it relates presently to one's personal association with eternity's divine norm. It must have a present application to reality. What is the reality of how you relate to Christ? The issue is not how we compare with him. It is not contrast that is sought, but contact. Those who relate to him dependently can avoid an emotional overdraft.

I pity the physically poor. They think wealth is the answer to their internal needs.

I pity the physically wealthy. They already know that money is not the answer to their internal needs.

The physically poor and/or rich who realize their internal insolvency and allow the proper divine deposit to be made in their life are on the road to happiness.

Wallace Johnson, one of the cofounders of Holiday Inn International, was once asked why, having independent wealth, he was so dependent on Christ. He answered, "When one has money, he realizes that is not where life's meaning is found."

John D. Rockefeller, Sr., observed, "The poorest man I know is the man who has nothing but money, and certainly some of the wealthiest men I have known have had very little money in the bank." The issue isn't income. It is internal upkeep.

It does little good in the search for happiness to lay up for yourself "treasures on earth." They become corrupted or get stolen. They get tarnished or taken.

Christ always stressed the value of personhood. Whether rich or poor, intellectual or ignorant, titled or unknown—all are persons. It is this basic nature we are to reverence and respect. This is more than the enshrinement of an ideal. It is the implementation of an aspiration. It is a frame of mind that can be maintained.

The poor in spirit realize their worth and how they work. We are very much like an expensive child's toy. All the parts and polish may be present, but it won't work without a battery. It must have an internal source of power. The values and virtues of life must have a supreme source of eternal power inserted. Like the battery, it is only utilized when the need for it is acknowledged. The poor in spirit have an awareness of such a need. Christ is that power cell.

Vitalized Values

It is readily observable that the world is like a giant shop window. Some practical joker has moved all the price tags around so that the valueless things have higher prices marked on them. The things of great value are rated low. Similarly, society seems to have its values all mixed up. We value the wrong things. Thus, we seek that which is garish rather than the Godly. We pursue the perishable rather than the permanent. We go after the gossamer instead of the good. It pays to check the price tags against the listing in the catalog— the Bible.

The poor in spirit have given up their desire for harmful and superficial things. They have assessed their values correctly. Having done so, they have invested in the things of greatest value. Their priorities are proper, and they are seeking first "the kingdom of God."

The poor in spirit are not inflated by egotism, not easily bruised, not always seeking their rights. They possess a resilience of spirit that keeps them from being crushed. Such persons are not disappointed because the world will not devote itself to making them happy. They are dependent upon an invisible means of support.

The poor in spirit do not rush by today to get to tomorrow. They are conscious of the value of the present. A right attitude about *now* is known to be an essential ingredient in happiness. Even in ancient Sanskrit it is noted:

> Look well to this one day, for in it and it alone is life. In the brief course of this one day lie all the varieties and realities of your existence; the pride of growth, the glory of action, the splendor of beauty.
> Yesterday is but a dream and tomorrow is but a vision. Yet each day, well-lived, makes every yesterday a dream of happiness and each tomorrow a vision of hope. Look well, therefore, to this one day, for in it and it alone is life.

The poor in spirit invest today wisely. They have resolved not to do anything today that will mess up tomorrow. They know sand can't run uphill in an hourglass, you can't unscramble an egg, and a pickle can never be a cucumber again.

The poor in spirit patiently wait on the Lord. They have made as their own this ageless prayer:

> O Lord, renew my strength now,
>   but if not now,
>   then tomorrow,
>   and if not tomorrow,
>   then help me to wait in hope
>   and somehow endure whatever happens in patience.
> Let me reach out to my brothers and sisters
>   who are struggling
>   in their own devastation and powerlessness
>   that they cannot change.
> Let us be patient with each other,
>   and help me to be patient with myself.

To acknowledge being poor in spirit is to take the first step toward perfection. James, the son of Mary and Joseph, urged his readers to be "perfect" (Jas. 1:4). The word he used does not hint at sinless perfection. It means to be mature, to reach a goal. Christ used the same word on the cross. It is translated, "It is finished" (John 19:30). He had reached his goal. His purpose had matured. The poor in spirit have taken a giant step in their journey to maturity. They are on their way to reaching their intended goal—to be conformed to the image of Jesus Christ.

No great journey has ever been completed without the first step being taken. No magnificent building has ever been constructed without the first stone being set. One doesn't reach maturity without starting. The attitude embodied in the expression "poor in spirit" is the first action leading to maturity.

Pride's Price

The poor in spirit are avoiding the pitfall of pride. This peril has been the sword of self-destruction on which many have fallen. It is the sultry, siren voice used to divert many from their course. Pride is the chain used to bind many to superficiality. It is a veil that clouds the vision of many.

Benjamin Franklin listed twelve virtues which he thought embodied traits of a good life. They are: temperance, silence, order, resolution, frugality, industry, sincerity, justice, moderation, cleanliness, tranquillity, chastity, and humility. Truly these are all vital life qualities. Note, however, that Franklin put humility last. Jesus put it first. Every list of sins in the Bible lists pride first. Pride is not just a flaw in the surface; it is a fracture in the foundation of life. "God resisteth the proud, but giveth grace unto the humble" (Jas. 4:6).

Pride is like the dome light in a car. When it is on, one can't see well. It has an internal blinding effect. It restricts one's vision. To be blinded by one's attitudes is tragic. Helen Keller was once asked by a thoughtless person, "Isn't it awful to be blind and not be able to see?" The poor in spirit have not had their eyes blinded by pride.

The saintly Jerome warned: "Beware of the pride of humility." False humility is even worse than pride. It actually is pride in disguise. Only the odor gives it away. It is a putrid personality trait. It stinks.

The poor in spirit are free from pride and vanity. They are transparent—you can see God through them.

Christ's ethic calling for persons to be "poor in spirit" is a moral code for heroes.

This code calls for unconditional surrender. When one does so, the assets of his conqueror become his own. The best thing that ever happened to Japan was its defeat in World War II. The conqueror became the benefactor. America's assets and abilities were used to reconstruct Japan. It has enjoyed unparalleled prosperity as a result. In unconditional surrender to the lordship of Christ, one gains his supervision and supply. The abandonment of arrogant pride is the first move toward personal reconstruction.

There are various kinds of pride. One kind is very good and one very bad. Be sure the kind you have is the type that enables you to keep your chin up and not your nose. False

pride, egotism, is destructive. It can cause one to pass rapidly
from a hero to a zero. On the shelf beside the volumes of
Who's Who could be another entitled *Who Was Who!*

There is a fable that is illustrative of fact.

A woodpecker was pecking away energetically on the trunk
of a dead tree. Lightning struck the tree and splintered it.
The woodpecker flew away, unharmed. Upon looking back
where the dead tree had been, the proud bird declared, "Look
what I did!"

The poor in spirit know that Christ spoke of great accomplishments and the source of their completion. "The things
that are impossible with man are possible with God" (Luke
18:27). Our splendid, splintered trees result from supernat-
ural assistance. The proud ignore it. The poor in spirit acclaim
it.

The poor in spirit do not use self-glorifying speech. Samson
killed a lion and said nothing about it. Some who kill a mouse
boast of it. Ours should not be conversation about what we
have done for the Lord, but of what he has done for us.

The poor in spirit when most impressed are Christ-
possessed.

One's greatest fault is to be conscious of none. A fault
that is recognized is half-corrected. Impudent pride blinds
one to faults that need correcting.

Spiritual poverty is the best kind. The worst kind is described in this poem by Debbie Groves.

> Poverty is having many acquaintances
>   and not knowing any of them.
> Poverty is having so many clothes that
>   you "haven't a thing to wear."
> Poverty is eating so well
>   you have to think about going on a diet.
> Poverty is having every pill imaginable
>   to cure your body's ills because
>   you "can't afford to be sick."
> Poverty is parents who keep their marriage together
>   for your sake.

Poverty is being loaded down with toys
   at birthdays and Christmas
   and then being bored silly
   because there's nothing to do.
Poverty is having two cars, three TVs, and a dishwasher
   and then "roughing it" by going camping
   to get away from it all.
Poverty is the day-to-day going from one building to the next
   and never stopping
   to see the beauty
   in the world outside.
Poverty is spending money
   on makeup, deodorants, talcs, and colognes,
   and still being worried
   about the image you are projecting.
Poverty is never being curious
   about the world around you,
   never wanting to explore it
   or the people in it.
Poverty is of the soul as well as the body.

The poor in spirit see themselves honestly as they are before God. This awakens a need for his love and forgiveness. They come with empty hands to receive the love which they can never earn, but which is theirs for the taking.

Lacking a mainspring, a watch, though beautiful, is worthless. A sundial without a gnomon, the iron finger of time, is useless. A ship with no rudder wanders aimlessly. The longest row of zeros adds up to nothing. When even the smallest number is added to the head of the row, the value changes. A life without Christ in charge of the control center is worthless, useless, aimless, and without its true value. When Christ becomes number one and is put first, he changes the value of life and gives it worth, usefulness, and direction. The poor in spirit have given him this position.

Some persons have made themselves their god, and their god has let them down. They then become a walking civil war. They are a committee of one, constantly embroiled in conflict. All persons need a god greater than any of us can ever be. The poor in spirit have dethroned self. They have ended the agony of their individual anarchy by enthroning Christ. They are then at peace. This contributes to one's avoiding an emotional overdraft.

Former United Nation's secretary-general, Dag Hammarskjold, made note of an attitude that typifies the poor in spirit.

> Vanity rears its ridiculous little head and holds up the distorting mirror in front of you for a mere instant, but one time is too many. It is at such times that you invite defeat and betray Him whom you serve. No man can do properly what he is called upon to do in this life unless he can learn to forget his ego and act as an instrument of God.

Such a moment of vanity occurred in the life of Billie Burke on a trans-Atlantic trip. She noted that a gentleman at the next table was having difficulty breathing because of a bad cold.

"Uncomfortable?" she queried sympathetically.

In return she received an affirmative nod.

"I'll tell you what to do for it," she responded. "Go back to your stateroom and drink a lot of orange juice. Take five aspirin tablets. Cover yourself with all the blankets you can find. Sweat the cold out. I know what I'm talking about. I'm Billie Burke of Hollywood."

The man smiled graciously and said, "Thanks; I'm Dr. Charles Mayo of the Mayo Clinic."

Pass Praise

Recognition and praise can flood a life and inundate it. If accolades are received by a person who becomes a receptacle for recognition, that can be devastating. If one realizes self to be a conductor of praise on its way to the supreme source, it energizes. In athletic, political, social, economic, and other circles, repetitious stories are recorded of persons who could not handle recognition because they did not know what to do with it. The poor in spirit invest it to gain eternal interest.

Upon receiving compliments and achieving success, one should engage in a period of prayer-praise. Thus, there is occasion to rejoice over accomplishments and at the same time to remove the threat of ego inflation. The doer does not become an end in self, but a transfer of praise into glorification.

It has been said that the most difficult grace of all is the grace of receiving. More precisely defined, the grace of receiving praise is burdensome. To relieve yourself of the burden, pass it on to the giver of every good and perfect gift. In this manner, one is giving rather than receiving. It is, after all, more blessed to give than receive. It is a blessing to receive, but it is more blessed to give. When praise is received and relayed to the Lord, one is doubly blessed and not burdened.

Humanity's haughtiness received Shakespeare's remonstration: "But man, proud man, Drest in a little brief authority, . . . Plays such fantastic tricks before high heaven As make the angels weep" *(Measure for Measure)*. The proud preening of one's ego must be highly offensive to the heavenly hosts that did not seek eminence above God. If they did not, neither should we.

Improper, inordinant pride is insulation between God and man. One cannot properly pray "thine is . . . the glory" and not acknowledge all praise to be as unto the Lord.

Proper Perspective

Most things that cause ego flights are short-lived. When Charles DeGaulle was informed of the fall of the world-influencing Khrushchev, he exclaimed, "Sic transit gloria mundi" —"Thus passes away the glory of the world."

Napoleon capsuled this fading fame properly: "I am doing now what will fill thousands of volumes in this generation. In the next, one volume will contain it all. In the third, a paragraph, and in the fourth, a single line."

The apostle Peter made note of the same fact: "For all flesh is as grass, and all the glory of man as the flower of grass" (1 Pet. 1:24).

Clemenceau, one of a half-dozen giants of World War I, paused to view the grave he had dug for himself. He commented to his secretary, "Take a look at it. There, in a nutshell, is all you can say about me—a hole in the ground and a great deal of noise about nothing."

The poor in spirit have a proper perspective of time and eternity. They possess a balanced sense of propriety. Egomania does not consume them. They are neither greedy for personal glory nor proud of individual praise. Bouquets gathered in time are displays intended for eternity. Pride holds them so tightly they wilt.

There has never been a supremely happy egotist. There is always the fear of failure, resulting in criticism. An air of anxiety is associated with every activity. Apprehension of not being accepted or approved of creates neuroses. Tension builds when praise is not lavished. No group of persons can feed the insatiable appetite of an inflated ego. Indirect appeals for ego appetizers alienate friends. No one likes to be around a vanity vacuum. There is always the danger of being sucked in.

The cavernous capacity of a narcissist for recognition is like a bottomless well. The deep longing of the life cannot be filled. Such a life perpetually senses a feeling of emptiness. This longing is often misunderstood as being a need for recognition. It is, but it is not recognition of the individual that is needed. It is recognition by the individual of a God worthy of praise that is needed.

A consuming lust for self-elevating flattery depletes one's friends. They too become anxious that they will fail to please the object of their veneration. No amount of acclaim will placate the palate of the proud. Such a one starves all associates of reasonable recognition and robs God of the glory due him. They compose an abyss of acclaim. Everyone who comes near fears he will fall in.

The spiritually proud make reasonable people feel like a piece of lint in their black-wool world. They attract persons and then pick them. Spiritual pride offends and alienates rational people. This is recycled by the spiritually proud as an indication of their own genuineness and goodness.

Such persons take great pride in being offensive. To them offending people is as spiritually virtuous as collecting scalps was heroic to Indians. The more offended persons left strewn in their wake, the more pious they feel. They consider a repelled person a reward for righteousness. These individuals need to exercise caution lest Satan tempt them to be proud of not being proud.

Poverty's Product

Although the Beatitudes themselves offer benefits, not even they encourage response for selfish motives. They simply identify the natural results of a life lived by their standards. Every resulting benefit is a natural consequence, not an affixed reward. Jesus constantly criticized good acts done for selfish motives to gain applause or reward.

The saintly Francis Xavier expressed this principle in verse as follows:

> My God, I love Thee; not because
> I hope for heav'n thereby,
> Nor yet for fear that loving not
> I might forever die;
> . . . .
> Not with the hope of gaining aught,
> Not seeking a reward,
> But as thyself hast loved me,
> O ever loving Lord!
> E'en so I love Thee, and will love,
> And in Thy praise will sing,
> Solely because Thou art my God
> And my eternal King.

Each of the Beatitudes has three parts: a statement of happiness, the character involved, and a resulting consequence.

Being poor in spirit results in being a part of the kingdom of God. *For* begins the last half of each Beatitude. That word is a forceful particle in the New Testament. It could and per-

haps best should be rendered *because*. It stresses the logic of
what Christ says.

The Beatitudes are not characteristic of conduct calculated
for gain. The characteristic is the bud; the blessing is the
flower.

The poor in spirit, those who dethrone pride, glean a beautiful bouquet of blessings. In this masterful message Christ's
teaching is diametrically opposed to the world's norm. He
offers an eternal, internal kingdom for a state of mind. There
is no alluding to external conquest or commercial gain.

The promise is immediate, however. He said that theirs
"Is the kingdom of heaven" (Matt. 5:3). He does not say
theirs "will be the kingdom of heaven." It is a present-tense
acquisition.

The kingdom of heaven refers more to a reign than a region.
He rules in minds and reigns over life-styles. The poor in
spirit are under his sovereignty. That means they can rely
on his provisions, protection, and power. He is theirs because
they are his. Consequently, the Beatitudes are doctrinally interesting as well as socially meaningful. They deal with Christ's
dominion over their domain. These are they who are a living
embodiment of Christ's prayer: "Thy will be done."

Their kingdom of heaven is the rule of Christ in their lives.
These teachings were designed to counteract the earthly view
of most persons. Jesus presented himself as the prophesied
king and the kingdom he offered as the prophesied kingdom.
The principles of the kingdom are far more than rules; they
are representative of the nature of the subjects. The result
of each attitude refers to an enriched and fulfilled life. This
is a result of unmerited gifts of God, not of persons earning,
meriting, or deserving his favor. Human achievement is not
the issue. Divine favor is. This, in part, explains why some
persons are supremely happy. This happiness is superior to
circumstances. Each of the eight attitudes couples with the
others to offer a combination that unlocks inner spiritual happiness. They are like an eight-rung ladder. Each step takes
one higher in happiness. In formula with each other, they

achieve an alchemy of spirit by which even bitter and grievous things are changed to blessedness.

Jesus said of the poor in spirit, "Theirs is the kingdom." "Theirs" is emphatic in the Greek. It is theirs and no others'. To possess the kingdom is to be possessed by the king. In this light, he exclaimed: O, the "well-being" of such ones. They are so "fortunate" that they are "to be congratulated." This kingdom status is "God's gift to you." Such persons are "joyous" and "fulfilled." All of these word meanings are found in the word used by Christ and translated *blessed*. Literally, these persons are supremely happy.

Those convicted of their spiritual poverty need reminders of their professed dependency. Following are some aids to assist one in maintaining a spirit of spiritual poverty.

Remember God's character as revealed in his Word. He is holy, just, loving, merciful, powerful, and present.

Be alert to occasions of pride. Some are success, achievement, victory, and accomplishment.

Forget those things which are behind, such as grief, guilt, gain, glory, gloat, and glamour.

Forever look to the cross. See its grace, compassion, forgiveness, meekness, and purity.

The Stipulation

BEAUTIFUL ATTITUDES

A tolerable play on words
  has virtue
If it helps one gain a word's
  true value.
Note that these masterful teachings
  of the Master
    are called
      the BE—atitudes
        not
        the DO—atitudes.
One must first BE
  before he can DO.
The Beatitudes
    are a pocket-sized biography
      of Christ.
He personified them.
He embodied them.
He was the Beatitudes incarnate.
None of us can live them alone.
Christ alone can live them in us
  as he is allowed to live in us.
Don't try to
  DO
    until you allow him to
      BE
        your Savior and Lord.

2
How to Enjoy Comfort
Even When Uncomfortable

Deep in the desert of the Hashimite Kingdom of Jordan
stands the remains of the Crusader fort of Kerak. Beautifully
located on the summit of a domed sand mountain in the ancient region of Moab, it commands the countryside. It consists
of seven concentric massive walls. Each wall is enveloped
within the other and separated by several yards. Each base
starts at about the top of the adjacent outer wall. Thus, if
an enemy were to breach an outer wall, he was met by other
equally or more formidable ones. Such a fortress castle
seemed invulnerable. It easily repelled many assaults. Its omi-
nous presence was a deterrent to many would-be attackers.
Kerak was the controlling factor regarding all surrounding
terrain.

The Crusaders built their forts so that each one was visible
from at least one other. Thus, they formed a network of supportive systems. Each could send aid to any other that gave
signs of distress. For Kerak or any fortress to fall, it must
be overwhelmed and defeated swiftly. The very composition
of this desert fortress made conquest unlikely if not impossible.

After having laid siege to the fort for several days, the forces
of Saladin were resting at a spring. They were encamped at
a small oasis near the base of the mountain, some distance
from the fort. One soldier noticed the peculiar markings of
a stray dog that came to drink at the spring. Soon thereafter
he noticed the same dog on the walls of the fort. Later he
observed the dog come to drink again. Soon he once again
saw the dog above on the massive walls. The warrior knew

there had to be a way for the dog to get in and out of the citadel.

When the dog next came to drink, he was watched and followed carefully. At the foot of the mountain he entered a cave. Hours later he emerged again on the walls. By association it was immediately concluded that this cave formed a tunnel leading into the innermost blockhouse. A short time later the soldiers of Saladin slithered through the tunnel into the heart of Kerak. The element of surprise enabled them to overwhelm the unsuspecting Crusaders. When they captured the heart of the stronghold, the countryside around the fort capitulated rapidly. A battle anticipated to be savage was relatively simple. When the core containing munitions, food, and other vital supplies was captured, the battle, for all practical purposes, was over.

The Beatitudes speak to the fortification of the inner person. It is the defense and resulting offense of the heart that Christ addresses. If the inner person is fortified and supplied, the person has cause to be supremely happy. If the inner person is invaded by corrupting forces, the outer actions are affected. Out of the heart come the issues of life.

Two hours before President Jimmy Carter took the oath of office on January 20, 1977, I had the pleasure of preaching the inaugural sermon. It was to be a private worship experience for an august assembly. In attendance were the president and Mrs. Carter and their relatives, vice-president and Mrs. Mondale and their relatives, the joint chiefs of staff and their families, the members of the Cabinet and their families, and the White House staff and aides. It was a meaningful historical moment. Shortly before the service began, I was silently praying and meditating on the Word of God. Vice-President Mondale's father-in-law, Dr. John Maxwell Adams, quietly approached me and said, "I see you are doing what the Quakers call 'centering down.'" This is a summary statement which simply means getting the inner person mobilized and harmonized. In the Beatitudes, Christ repeatedly promises blessings for persons who properly "center down" on the right factors.

Ambrose called these teachings "the paradoxes of Christ." Some seem superficially contradictory. When reviewed in light of Christ's intent, they are laws of logic and reason.

Christianity as Christ taught it is commendable. Realizing this, Albert Einstein commented, "It is Christianity as Christ taught it that is the cure for the world's ills today." The Beatitudes are a distillation of eternal truths as taught by the Master Teacher. If they will work for society it is because they will work in the life of individual components of that society. They are germane to this generation. They are a prescription for the present, waiting to be taken. They not only increase resistance to depleting and debilitating influences of life; they energize and make one supremely happy.

Mourn (pentheō) means to grieve with a grief which so consumes the whole being that it cannot be hidden—grief that manifests itself externally. It can mean sorrow, grief, or a painful event. Though penitent sorrow is involved, this encompasses all sorrow.

The Book of History, one of the Chinese classics, lists the "Five Happinesses." These are the ingredients they consider basic to happiness: long life, riches, soundness of body and serenity of mind, love of virtue, and an end crowning the life.

Unequivocally, these are assets in any life. Only a part of one hints at the elements Christ emphasized, however. There is no indication of happiness resulting from mourning. Christ said there is.

The Savior is a spiritual seismograph, sensing the needs of his subjects. He knows that mourning was inevitable and normal. His intent is to give it meaning and direction. It thus can become virtuous and advantageous. Pain can become profitable; grief can become gain. Often our disappointments are God's appointments. At first this seems impossible and impractical. The benefits are not immediately apparent. They are nevertheless inherent and can contribute to making one supremely happy.

Sorrow is inevitable; there is no option. To mourn is a

natural expression of sorrow. Our response to sorrow is optional.

The Beatitudes succeeded one another like links in a golden chain. This natural progression prompted Saint Chrysostom to comment of the second one: "We should mourn our stubborn pride."

Repentance Required

Christ's reference to those who mourn does not relate so much to an act as an attitude. He is not simply seeking a broken heart, but rather a contrite spirit. No honest person would insist that there is nothing in his life that should produce contrition or sincere repentance. A genuine attitude of change is repentance.

A British friend described this proper form of repentance to me in the following manner:

Before repentance, it is as though all persons are standing in a circle facing outward and holding hands. In the center of the circle is a large brilliant light. In this posture the arch necessary for forming the circle puts an uncomfortable strain on the arms of each as they must reach back slightly to clasp the hands of those adjacent. In addition, they have difficulty seeing their neighbors properly as they look straight ahead. Before them is their own shadow cast by the light. This is an awkward, discomforting position.

When one repents, he turns inward. Now he can comfortably see and more easily reach out to his neighbor. The shadow of self is gone, and the light enables him to see more clearly. Only stubborn pride will prevent one from changing to this more comfortable position. When one mourns pride and repents, changing his spiritual position, then he can be supremely happy.

It was a day of blessing when Sir Lancelot called himself the most unhappy of all knights. This bold acknowledgment was a moment of truth for the bold warrior. It prompted him to say, "My sin and my wickedness have brought me into great dishonour." His mourning lasted until day. The

singing of the birds somewhat comforted him. It was a day
of blessing when Queen Guinevere repented of her infidelity
and heard the voice of the king: "Lo! I forgive thee, as Eternal
God forgives: do thou for thine own soul the rest."

In the lives of countless millions, as in the lives of these
two, mourning can be most comforting. So much so that it
leads to supreme happiness.

Threefold comfort is suggested in the king's statement:
comfort resulting from being forgiven by the one wronged;
comfort resulting from being forgiven by God; comfort that
is potential from acceptance of forgiveness.

We should abuse neither our joys nor our sorrows. Excessive anguish is not the intent. Ours is not what Paul called
the "sorrow of the world." Such is self-indulgence. However,
when regulated properly, the furnace of affliction serves as
a "refiner's fire." Godly sorrow worketh repentance unto salvation. Sorrow with a purging purpose is profitable. It is
mourning with a meaning. It is not an end in itself, but a
means to an end.

Responsible Results

Mature mourning sobers judgment. It prompts people to
weigh values. Sorrow often summons self-denial and stimulates serviceability. Higher and nobler instincts are awakened
by it. Our mourning frequently reveals the true grace of others, prompting us to say, "I never knew people cared so
much." It solicits supportive strength.

Natural community-wide disasters that wreck lives and break
hearts most often bring people closer together. Even areas
that tend to be extremely exclusive and ultraprivate, such
as Beverly Hills in California, are drawn out by mutual sorrow.
Recent floods in that community resulted in new companionship. Neighbors who did not even know each other came to
the aid of others. Their occasion for mourning was an opportunity for comforting.

My wife was given a lovely gift of an assortment of various
exotic tea blends. Inadvertently, they were dropped. The iden-

tifying boxes containing each blend popped open, mixing the various bags. It was impossible to identify each because they all had the same tag. Only the box from which they came identified them. It was impossible to tell them apart until they were put in hot water. Many people are like that: You can't truly tell what they are like until they get in hot water. It is our response to crises that is more important than the event itself. If our mourning turns us in the right direction, it is most advantageous.

Sorrow is inevitable. God takes no pleasure in our grief. He will take part in it, however. His displeasure over our pain is indicated by his heavenly provisions: "God shall wipe away all tears from their eyes; and there shall be no more death, neither sorrow" (Rev. 21:4). His ultimate provision in the place of his sovereign rule will enable persons to "Enter thou into the joy of thy Lord" (Matt. 25:21).

Nevertheless, here in time the character of Christ himself typifies our plight. God had only one Son, and not even he was exempt from pain. Isaiah described him as "a man of sorrows."

Tolstoy's observation speaks well to this subject. "A man who lives a Christian life does not ascribe any great meaning to his joys, but looks on them as accidental phenomena which meet him in the path of life. And he does not look upon his sufferings as something that ought not to be. He looks on them as indispensable phenomena of life, like friction at work."

Pebble Beach on the coast of California is a lovely area that typifies the advantages of friction. Ceaseless waves thunder ashore and dash the beach. The pitiless pounding of the waves tosses and grinds the stones together. They are dashed against the rugged, ageless cliffs. Unabated, this action goes on year after year. The resulting round, polished stones are collected by tourists as ornaments. Near Pebble Beach is a quiet cove. A natural formation serves as a breakwater. Sheltered by the cliff are numerous stones. They are unsought and unwanted. They have been spared the wear caused by the waves. They have remained rough and unpolished. Their potential beauty has not been developed. Life's buffeting also has a refining effect on human life. It can be friction causing fascinating features in a life.

Renoir, the famous French impressionist painter, suffered severely from the agony caused by rheumatism. Every stroke of the brush was purchased at the price of pain. Anguish wrote with distinct lines on his face. He had to sit while painting to help avoid pain. Renoir endured this agony to produce many masterpieces. He captured rare beauty on canvas. Once a friend inquired of him, "Why do you continue to torture yourself?"

Wisely, Renoir replied, "The pain passes, but the beauty remains!"

The beauty remaining from our mourning can minister to many. The elixir it extracts can comfort others.

The Irish poet Thomas Moore was the possessor of a warm, spritely spirit. A distinct development in his poetry can be traced and associated with events in his life. His oldest daughter's death had a profound effect on him. Later grief once again visited him as a result of his youngest daughter's death. Travail troubled his life for months. He spoke of nearly being overwhelmed by his grief. He tried retreating from reality. As an attempt to escape, he sought solace in solitude. His reflections on the reality of heaven brought consolation. He expressed his new peace of mind and spoke of its source in his hymn with which many have identified.

> Come, ye disconsolate, where'er ye languish,
> Come to the mercy seat, fervently kneel;
> Here bring your wounded hearts, here tell your anguish;
> Earth has no sorrow that heav'n cannot heal.

The undesired friction of sorrow caused mourning, resulting in undeniable comfort.

A diamond is a bit of ordinary earth that has passed through an extraordinary experience. Great treasures of oil are stored beneath the trackless waste of desert sands. Despise not the desert of sorrow; develop its resources.

Robert Louis Stevenson's works have enriched the lives of many. His classic work is identified among the best of all ages. He described as follows the crucible out of which it came:

> For fourteen years I have not had a day of real health. I have awakened sick and gone to bed weary. I have done my work unflinchingly. I have written in bed and out, when torn by coughing and when my head swam for weariness. The battle goes on. Ill or well is a trifle, so long as it goes on. I was made for conflict. The powers that be have willed my battlefield shall be this dingy, inglorious one of the bed and the medicine bottle!

He did not whine or recline, but he did incline his heart in a productive direction. His indomitable will resulted in indispensable work. The shadow of Stevenson's sorrow has brightened many. Without a storm there can be no rainbow. The rays of hope that shine through sorrow bring out some of life's greatest brilliance.

An Irish baby born in 1819, Joseph Scriven, was to walk a road of shadows and sorrows. Problems and perplexities plagued his path. Some mused that apart from his friendship with Christ, he would have failed mentally.

One of the brightest spots in his life was a beautiful young fiancée. The love of these two for each other brought joy to others who observed its effects. It was at this point that sorrow reached a flood tide in his life. His beloved was accidentally drowned shortly before they were to be wed. His overwhelming grief caused him to leave his beloved Ireland to settle in Canada.

His life was blanketed by this and other burdens. One night in 1855, his burden rolled away. Through prayer, he defeated despondency. His petition for comfort was accompanied by a commitment to serve Jesus Christ. The night became day; the shadow became substance; and joy flooded his arid soul. This rush of elation prompted him to immediately pen his pleasure. Quickly, he wrote a poem which has since become a hymn that has cheered many. It contains these words:

> What a friend we have in Jesus,
>   All our sins and griefs to bear!
> What a privilege to carry
>   Ev'rything to God in prayer!
> Oh, what peace we often forfeit,
>   Oh, what needless pain we bear,
> All because we do not carry
>   Everything to God in prayer!

Friction had filtered his faith. The bud of sorrow had produced the blossom of comfort. He became supremely happy.

As the promising career of George Matheson was just beginning, he was told by his doctor that he would soon be blind. This disturbing news altered the course of his life.

A person of character, he told his fiancée and gave her a graceful occasion to break their engagement. She did. Understandably, this afforded him great sorrow. This was vitally important, but not so much as his response. Bitterness, which is fermented sorrow, was an option. Resentment, which is sorrow soured, was another alternative. Neither of these was his response. These twin tragedies deepened his devotion to Christ. Out of the "furnace of affliction" came these words:

> O love that wilt not let me go,
>   I rest my weary soul in thee,
> I give thee back the life I owe,
>   That in thine ocean depths its flow
> May richer, fuller be!

Raw reality had refined his life. He could not control his circumstances. Neither did he let his circumstances control him. They did not abuse him, but he did use them. His "richer, fuller" life was purged and prepared so he could be supremely happy.

It is not God's purpose to comfort us in our mourning to make us comfortable, but "that we may be able to comfort them which are in any trouble, by the same comfort wherewith we ourselves are comforted of God" (2 Cor. 1:4).

Chaplain Wyatt Willard approached the hospital bed of a young sailor who had lost his left leg. The bitter amputee barked out, "Well, chaplain, start cheering me up! You're a Navy specialist; so do your stuff." Try as he did, the chaplain felt helpless to comfort the abrasive sailor.

A young marine corporal in a wheelchair rolled up to his bed the following day. A giant, generous grin lit up the face of the double amputee marine. Not sarcasm, but a faint smile was the response. Suffering had met suffering. The battle between despair and courage had been enjoined. Courage brought comfort; despair was defeated.

That afternoon Chaplain Willard was met with an accusing smile and a quizzical comment. "Chaplain," the sailor said, "that was some trick—sending me that marine amputee. But it worked, I guess. The nurse said I have become a pretty decent fellow."

His paroxysm of grief had become his prism of gain.

Not only does our grief enable us to meet other's needs, but others are equipped to meet ours. Abraham Lincoln, the Great Emancipator, brought comfort to many. His life was strewn with sorrow. Lincoln found comfort to be reciprocal. He noted, "When I left Springfield, I was not a Christian. When I buried my son, the severest trial of my life, I was not a Christian. But when I went to Gettysburg and saw the graves of thousands of soldiers, I then and there consecrated myself to Christ. Yes, I do love Jesus." The compound mourning resulting from the grief of Gettysburg brought eternal comfort to Mr. Lincoln.

In an earlier agricultural era, a device called a *tribulum* was used to beat grain in order to divide the wheat from the chaff. Our word *tribulation* has the same root as this agricultural instrument. Tribulation often threshes chaff from our lives, enabling us to become supremely happy.

Dark velvet is often the material used to display brilliant diamonds. Days of despair have frequently formed a background for some of life's greatest joys. Comfort can come from the caldron of calamity.

There is also special comfort available to those who mourn

because of their compromising character, calloused conduct, and capitulation of convictions.

When a person realizes inequities within his life and genuinely desires to change, he can. This change can bring great comfort. This comfort is brought about when there is labor of love, patience of hope, and work of faith.

Dereliction leads to despondency. Diligence leads to delight. Compromise corrodes character. Consistency confirms character.

The life often needs purging. Sorrow is a means of accomplishing it. Repressed sorrow can actually be fatal. Expressed sorrow is therapeutic. Pent-up grief can be debilitating. Tear ducts are one form of escape valve for grief. It can often be healthy to cry. Certain circumstances merit tears. Tears can release physical tension associated with grief. Likewise, there has to be a release for trouble resulting from guilt.

Spiritual mourning is a symptom suggesting the need of cleansing. It may be an acknowledgment of a personal lacking. It can be the portal to consolation. Conscience can be cleansed from guilt via mourning. It can be a guilt release. When it is, a person is blessed, adjusted, made stable. Mourning should be a means to an end. The end is cleansing resulting in comfort.

Catharsis is from the Greek word meaning to purge or cleanse. A spiritual catharsis can be a final filter leading to fidelity and faith. If the sorrow is over sin, not over getting caught, then our mourning is grief, not a grievance. Godly sorrow worketh repentance unto salvation.

It is not the mourning expressed in tears that cleanses spiritually. It is an inclination of the heart toward Christ as expressed by mourning over guilt that enables him to cleanse. He is the agent of cleansing. Mourning may be the avenue of expression associated with it. This varies in its expression with different people.

Comforted? They that mourn shall be comforted, said Christ. It is as though Christ and the world not only have different standards, but a different vocabulary. The world's concept of mourning is that it is the most distasteful of emotions and should be guarded against at all cost. Persons seek to ward it off by diverse means. It is to the world unmitigated disaster. It is looked upon with resentment and suspicion. The world seeks to build defenses to protect against it.

Christ acknowledged it as unavoidable and inescapable. He faced it as a fact of life that cannot be avoided. He considered it to be raw material for unique blessings. In the light of faith, Jesus welcomed it as a spiritual opportunity. There is no hint anywhere in his teachings that pain, suffering, and sorrow are to be sought as virtues within themselves. He merely acknowledges their inevitability and shows how to respond constructively.

"Comfort ye, comfort ye my people" (Isa. 40:1) rang refreshingly in the ears of citizens of the Old Testament era. Lives were buttressed by King David's reminder "Thou art with me; thy rod and thy staff, they comfort me" (Ps. 23:4). Although sorrow is not sought, comfort is craved. It comes only to those who experience an encounter that occasions it. Meaningful mourning produces contributing comfort.

Comforted is a very strong word with rich meaning. Later Christ said, "I will pray the Father and he shall send you another Comforter" (John 14:16). The Greek word for *comforter* is *Parakletos* or, as anglicized, *paraclete. Comforted* comes from the same English root as *comforter* or *paraclete.* Comforted is the passive verb *parakalein* meaning to comfort or console.

It is the word that was used to summon an ally, a helper, a tutor, an adviser, a counselor, or a witness. These qualities are available to those who mourn. They are assets in the hour of adversity.

It is the word used to invite one to a banquet. Heaven's bounty is spread before those who seek spiritual nourishment in their moment of mourning. The believer is invited to be nourished by a heavenly host.

It is the word meaning to exhort and encourage. In the hour of crisis there is an internal resource available to those who avail themselves of it. The Bible, God's Word, serves as his voice to reassure, inspire, hearten, and incite hope.

"Blessed are they that mourn, for they shall be *paracleted.*" They shall have an ally, a tutor, a helper, an adviser, a counselor, and a witness. They are invited to feast. They are exhorted and encouraged in their hour of mourning.

The Latin word *comforted* has two parts, *Com,* meaning together with, and *fort,* meaning strength. It denotes "bring strength together." In comfort, Christ comes to our side and shares his strength. This is the comfort offered to those who mourn. Apart from him there is no consolation. With him, even in sorrow one can be supremely happy.

The word *comfort* suggests strengthening, not soothing. It does not suggest an armchair. The root meaning is to make strong, to fortify. Therefore, don't ask for immunity from sorrow; ask for strength.

This comfort is not designed for or available to those who are rebelliously discontented, regretfully sorry over worldly loss, repining because of a melancholy disposition, or remorseful over wounded pride.

In seeking comfort, check your motive. Analyze the reason for needing it. If one of the above is the stimulus, it is not comfort that is needed; it is contrition.

This comfort is intended for and accessible to those who are regretful over offending God, repentant under God's discipline, responsive to God's grace, or related to God by faith.

To be under his reign is to benefit from his resources.

The Sight

WHAT HE SAW

Jesus SAW the multitude.
He saw them,
   not in the sense that he beheld them.
      Rather, he comprehended them.
The sight and the plight of the multitude
      prompted this matchless manifesto.
Jesus was presenting himself
         as the prophecied King
            and the Kingdom he offered
            as the prophecied Kingdom.
The principles he propounded
   are far more than rules.
They are representative of
   the nature of the inhabitants.
This new nature
   results from unmerited gifts from God
      not as a result of human achievement.
This new nature results in
   an enriched and fulfilled life.

WHAT HE SAID

"He opened his mouth . . ."
  has little to do with
    diction, inflection, phonation, or techniques of speech.
If a teenager were transliterating this it would be,
"He opened his heart to them."
Others might say,
  "He laid bare his soul."
An athlete would say,
  "He got on the gut level."
All hint at what he did.
He gave us the characteristics of
  citizens of the Kingdom.
This was the Sinai of the Savior.
The Law was accompanied by thunder and lightning
  that frightened the people away.
His logic was accompanied by love and light
  that drew people to him.
He spoke with authority
  and uncovered his heart
    in this his
      "Magna Charta of the Kingdom of heaven."

3
How to Settle the Family Estate

The pursuit of happiness for many people ends in a freakish traffic jam. Motors keep accelerating, but nobody can move. The engines are powerful, but confusion and congestion keep them from progressing. This has caused many people to forsake their quest for happiness and wrap themselves in a cocoon of cynicism.

Yale's president, Dr. Kingman Brewster, referred to cynicism as the key threat around college campuses today. Is there an antidote? He suggests five ingredients:

Happiness is more than material well-being.

Conscience is more than simple fear.

Love is more than sex.

Moral authority is more than political power.

Community is more than organization.

Reality reveals that not everyone is going to possess an abundance of physical goods. If happiness is dependent upon relating to material goods, a right attitude must be developed. The sum total of our substance may not be increased substantially, but our attitude toward material goods can be channeled. It is our attitude that Christ addresses in the Beatitudes. Attitude is the arena in which the battle for happiness is won or lost.

A Princeton, New Jersey, psychologist, Dr. Herbert M. Greenberg, has done revealing study in this field. His findings are based on interviews with more than 250,000 employees of four thousand firms. Included was every job category and educational group from every part of the country.

His findings revealed that 80 percent of all workers at all

levels are unhappy and frustrated. Imagine it; four out of every five persons are unhappy. One of America's biggest markets today is for happiness.

A primary reason for this is persons have a greed for things they can't obtain in sufficient quantities. An associated reason is that those who do secure them do not find any security in them. There is a wonderful line in the play *Alfie,* in which a man who is lonely because of the death of his wife confesses that he is unhappy. In effect, he says, "I pity poor people who are unhappy because they think money will help." Acquisitions and acquaintances will not help—attitude will.

Pliny the Elder, a famous Roman writer, once noted, "The only certainty is that nothing is certain." Modern observers have concluded that there is nothing real about real estate. It is easily lost or destroyed. Life's perils need not disillusion us, however. Stability is not in substance but in attitude. You have to believe.

> You have to believe in happiness
> Or happiness never comes.
> I know that a bird chirps nonetheless,
> When all that he finds is crumbs.
> You have to believe that the buds will bloom,
> Believe in the grass in the days of snow.
> Ah, that's the reason the bird can sing—
> On his darkest day, he believes in spring.
> You have to believe in happiness.
> It isn't an outward thing.
> The spring never made the song, I guess,
> As much as the song, the spring.

Meek (praüs) means one who is meek not because he can't help himself, but because of confidence of infinite eternal resources. It is equanimity of spirit that is neither elated nor cast down. It is persons who are mild, gentle, tender, pleasant. It means to calm that which is irritated or excited—to be under control.

Aristotle saw meekness as a fulcrum between two extremes. One was excessive anger and the other the lack of anger.

He saw it as always being angry at the right time about the right things, and never being angry at the wrong time about the wrong things. Too much heat can melt metal. Too little will fail to temper it and give it strength. Likewise, there must be balance in one's temperament if there is to be strength of character. Imbalance causes a personality flaw.

Meekness, as taught at Mount Beatitude University, referred to mastery by the Master. It does not allude to weakness. It is self-control, not spinelessness; positive humility, not negative timidity; a spirit under control of Christ, not a shrinking soul.

Christ depicted that which he taught. He demonstrated a balance between cowardice and recklessness resulting in controlled courage. It enables one to avoid a hot head or cold feet by maintaining a warm heart. "Thy will be done . . ." is exhibit "A" of meekness. Only the genuinely strong can be truly meek. Others are afraid to be. Only confidence in one's resources and reasoning can produce meekness. It is an exceptional strength.

The meek get more out of themselves. They are not overindulgent of self. Neither are they afraid to enjoy the simple, inherent delights of life. They are calm and confident.

The meek have control over themselves. It is manifest in long-suffering. Such persons are willing to leave their case before the eternal tribunal. There is no nervousness regarding the ultimate disposition of the case.

Meekness is love with enough muscle to quell anger's revolt and restrain a violent temper. Enough strength is shown to stimulate lethargy and laziness. Ego equilibrium is seen at its best in the meek. It is power blended with gentleness, disciplined with strength. It is seen in a person provoked but controlled. This control does not result from inability to defend oneself, but is dictated by logic and reason that suggests use of higher facilities than temper or muscle.

The environment takes control of the person who does not have control of self. St. Augustine noted, "Dost thou wish to possess the earth? Beware, lest the earth possess thee."

Blessed, adjusted, and stable is the person who has brought all of his drives under control. The reins are off the intemperate. Their internal guidance system is malfunctioning.

Weakness is yielding to our nature; meekness is conquering it. The meek's cosmos consists of more than his ego. Self is not center stage in the life of the meek. Such a life has room for others and different opinions.

True meekness is in perfect harmony with vitality, aggressive pursuit of purpose, and dynamic energy. Jesus was known as a man of "meekness and gentleness." Yet, he had enough muscle and mettle to cleanse the Temple and rebuke the religious leaders of his day.

Doormat Dispositions

To be meek does not mean to have a doormat disposition. It does not refer to a person with a low self-image. In no way does it suggest abdication of personhood. Conversely, it implies the fulfillment of it. The dynamic leader Moses was spoken of as being meek. Nothing in his conduct suggests a cowering character. His was a towering temperament.

Meekness is the easiest of the virtues to counterfeit. Many blurred imitations of it are offered. It may be a tepid temperament mothered by cowardice and fathered by compromise. Often it is a consequence of lack of conviction. It may simply symbolize a sluggish soul. This synthesis only capitulates and complains. It is never assertively productive. Like all other artificial acts, it is lacking in creative capacity. It is disguised weakness, not meekness.

The meek do not make selfish demands; yet they have boldness in asserting discerning desires. Being meek does not keep one from having inflexible determination regarding convictions. Meekness should never be confused with pacifism or identified with nonresistance. True meekness has to do with motivation as well as method. It has its origin in Godlikeness and is pure in purpose. Pacifism often relates to selfish, personal ambition. With the meek, personal profit is not paramount.

The word *meek* means more than being abject, servile, cast down in spirit, devoid of hope, or emotionally low. Many people think in such a frame of reference when they hear the word. It is because of this misconception that they cannot understand how such persons can ever receive the blessing promised in the third Beatitude.

Controlled Character

In ancient times, the word translated *meek* was used to describe the taming of a wild horse. When a desert-bred horse was saddle-broken and bridled, the word for *meek* was used to describe the act. The animal was still physically powerful, had a bold temperament, and a strong will. The difference was simply that all of these assets were controlled. Such an animal was bridled and the reins put in the hands of its new master. That is a graphic description of one whose temperament is truly meek. God does not rob him of his personality, make void his mentality, or mutate his individuality. He takes these gifts he gave in the first place and directs them. The control factor is the new ingredient in such a life. To be meek is to respond to the reins. It enables one to receive an inheritance of inestimable worth.

By listening to jockeys and horse trainers, we can learn the applied meaning of meekness. The winning horse is the "meekest on the track." This is the horse most under control. He has his own body under control; fatigue has not mastered it. He is the horse that responds most quickly to the jockey's guidance. The stubborn, self-willed fractious horse seldom is a winner.

Meekness is a vertical, not a horizontal, virtue. It relates to how we stand before God, not to how we stand with people.

A parallel can be seen in athletics. A player is under the supervision and instruction of his coach. The coach is wiser and more experienced and has a better vantage point. He is more capable of controlling the game. The athlete who best responds to his signals is the meekest player on the team. He may also be the best, biggest, and most successful. If so, it is because he has allowed his energies and efforts to be coordinated through his coach with everything else. He is constructively controlled.

To be meek is to be under God's control—to be teachable, coachable, and responsive to his rules. Thus, one is alive to his potential. If a person is unproductive, it is not because of meekness, but rather because of weakness. One's highest potential is reached when he is meekest—that is, most under control.

In America the word *strong* often evokes the image of steel. It is strong but inflexible. In the Orient the substance that is used to depict strength is water. Water is our idea of weakness. The Oriental observes the patient quality of water. It will shape itself to fit its container. Patiently, it waits. Suppose it is restrained by a dam. It takes the shape of the lake and waits. If an opening occurs in the dam, it moves slowly through it. Persistently it continues its controlled flow. In the process it erodes and enlarges its outlet. This controlled process continues persistently until at last it overpowers its restraint, the dam, and runs free. Water is strength because it is patient enough to be controlled until it can control.

The meek are not immediately frustrated by circumstances. They do not fight and struggle against their environment. An opportunity is sought for controlled expression. When managed action is possible, it is taken in the most positive and productive manner.

Meekness implies persistence as well as patience. The character of the water is not changed by its container. Its strength is not dissipated by delay. Neither are the meek dismayed or defeated by conditions and time. They are under control.

Handel's Happiness

As an old man, George Frederick Handel could have wasted his days in despair. Frequently his fertile mind flitted from memories of a glorious past to the hopeless despair of the present. A stooped-shouldered old man, he was often seen shuffling through the dark streets of London. For four decades he had written music that had thrilled the city and many others. He had received the accolades of England's crowned heads and the praise of the Continent's nobility. He had been bathed in honors.

Things changed abruptly. The court society turned on him without explanation. Street gangs broke up his operas. His small fortune was gradually depleted. He was soon reduced to abject poverty.

His health broke. The pressures mounted. A cerebral hemorrhage resulted in paralysis of his right side. He could neither write nor walk. The medical community gave him no hope of recovery. He was a broke and broken old man. He was depleted, but not defeated.

Handel went to Aix-la-Chapelle to take hot baths in hope of finding help. He was warned that staying in the scalding waters longer than three hours at a time would kill him. So desirous was he of healing that he stayed as long as nine hours. Inert muscles that had begun to atrophy were stimulated. His limbs took on new life. The paralysis passed, and soon he began to walk. It was a phenomenal recovery. That which was unexpected by the doctors was not unanticipated by the composer.

With renewed vigor, he resumed his work. His exhilaration resulted in the rapid production of four operas. His new success was met with renewed acclaim. The flower that flourished soon faded. Unexpectedly, his health once again failed.

To further complicate his plight, his longtime patroness, Queen Caroline, died. His drastic reduction of income was accompanied by a bitter British winter. The inflated costs of fuel required so much of the public's resources that they could little afford to go to the opera. His potentially busy schedule was cancelled. His income was depleted, and his savings were soon used up. His mounting debt distracted his attention and quieted his creative genius. From all appearances he was defeated by debt, disease, and despair.

He, as others, mused as to why God would be so cruel as to restore his unique skills only to snatch them away again.

Was this a hoax to end all hope?

One evening, as he returned from his purposeless walk through the cold streets, he found a package in his room. After he wiped away the tears caused by the icy winds, he tore open the package. It contained a musical score entitled "A Sacred Oratorio." Soaring hope slumped when he saw the name of its author, Charles Jennens. Some would have considered this second-rate poet presumptuous to ask the masterful Handel to compose an oratorio from it. The postscript, "The Lord gave me the Word," appeared a bit bold.

Handel thumbed through the pages. His indifference was arrested by such expressions as "He was despised and rejected of men . . ." "He looked for someone to have pity on Him, but there was no man; neither found He any comfort in Him." His kindred spirit caught fire. This was something with which the musician could identify.

"He will give thee rest . . ." and related lines renewed hope and gave birth to reason.

"I know that my Redeemer liveth . . ." "Rejoice . . . Hallelujah." This lightened his load and brightened his road.

Compatibility of spirit caused a combustible rekindling of his productive prowess. A responsive cord had been struck. The fertile furrows of his mind began to sprout with seeds of sweetest song. He began to write rapidly. Page after peerless page was rapidly produced. Unbelievable speed produced pages of inspiring ideas.

All through the night he wrote. Ceaselessly, he continued to chart score after score. The next day his manservant found him still busy at work. Choosing not to disturb him, he quietly left the breakfast tray. Upon returning at noon, he found the tray untouched.

For days the servant fretted over the composer as he refused food. Only occasionally would he stop and stride back and forth across the room flailing his arms up and down. Then he would rush back and resume writing.

When in exhaustion he concluded the work with the "Queen of Christian musical climaxes," the "Hallelujah Chorus," tears were streaming down his cheeks. He said to his servant, "I did think I did see all Heaven before me and the great God himself!"

Uncompromisingly, and uncomplainingly, he had labored for twenty-three uninterrupted days. He collapsed and fell into a seventeen-hour sleep of exhaustion. On a nearby table lay the score of what is unquestionably the greatest oratorio ever composed, *Messiah.*

The meek left us a priceless inheritance. Being controlled, he contributed. His brain was bridled. His reason had been reined by the Master. No weak character would have endured the agony of aloneness, the arduousness of sleeplessness, and abstinence from food required to create such continuity as this masterpiece possesses.

Obedient Origin

Anne Sullivan, the tutor of Helen Keller, noted, "I saw clearly that it was useless to try to teach her language or anything else until she learned to obey me. I have thought about it a great deal. The more I think, the more certain I am that obedience is the gateway through which knowledge, yes, and love, do enter the mind of a child."

Obedience is another word for control. The obedient individual is controlled. We have failed to inherit many of life's greatest blessings because of our obstinate disobedience to the will of God. Only as our stubborn will consents to constructive control can it find happiness.

Inherit the earth? The meek! That is contradictory to all appearances. At best, some assert, it must be a reference to the millennial reign of Christ. Most persons prefer to think this is a dispensational promise pertinent to some distant day. It will be fulfilled in a literal sense during that earthly enthronement of Christ. However, the believer does not have to wait for a distant date.

The word for *inherit* or *enjoy* means the same as the word for *possess.* The *heir* is the person who will inherit the land— the *inheritor* is the possessor. The word *possess* is often the legal equivalent to *enjoy*. In law, you *enjoy* certain rights when you *possess* them.

To enjoy something, one does not have to have title to it. A jewel-bedecked mandarin allowed a wise old man to behold the beauty of his treasure. The old man followed him through the street bowing and thanking him for his jewels. "What does this mean?" asked the mandarin. "I never gave you any of my jewels."

"No," he replied, "but you have let me look at them yourself, so the only difference between us is that you have the trouble of watching them; and that is an employment I don't much desire." To him possession was in appreciation for their beauty, not in possession of their title. He had inherited their aesthetic value without having to keep them in a vault. He possessed the pleasure, although not the property.

One person holds title to a tract of land. He sees only the monetary value to the property which he possesses. It is his by deed and is a resource. The person whose mind is controlled by Christ can see inherent in the same landscape all the beauty of God's handiwork. His aesthetic nature is fed by it. One has title to the land; the other has possession of the landscape.

In this vein, we all have a wonderful inheritance. I am personally very wealthy. I have inherited a beautiful, virtually endless white-sand beach at Jekyll Island, Georgia. There is a trackless estate of magnificent mountains in North Carolina which I inherited. There is a matchless marsh in Louisiana I count among my inheritance. The vast plains of Montana are mine. I cherish the cliff-lined coast of Oregon as a priceless part of my inheritance. Not to be overlooked are the lovely lakes of Michigan. Those are but a few of the splendid landscapes which I have inherited. I have possessed them. I treasure their scenic splendor. They have enriched my life. No title to them could do more for me than has been done. I simply do not have the stewardship responsibility that goes with the title. They are my resources for which I have no managerial responsibility.

"The earth is the Lord's and the fulness thereof" (Ps. 24:1). Any one of his children can enjoy his creation, knowing that he has said "All things . . . are mine" (John 16:15). Being joint heirs with Christ gives us an inheritance of inestimable value. Though we may own nothing, we possess everything. The mighty may inhabit the earth, but the meek inherit it. It has been bequeathed by the heavenly Father. They who use the world rightly possess it. Most persons have disinherited themselves from what God intended to be ours. The meek—that is, those who are God-tempered as well as God-tamed—have the capacity of enjoying their inheritance.

It appears that the meek might actually take title to the land after the greedy have killed themselves trying to get the deed to it.

To travel in Switzerland is to drive through a land of unimaginable beauty. It is one country that truly exceeds its best billing.

Late one August we were motoring from Zurich, Switzerland, to Milan, Italy. It was a brilliant day. We drove South toward Zug. The crisp, fresh air was a stimulus to the mind. The persons who comprised our party were warm and expressive. A buoyant attitude prevailed.

As we passed through Arth, we started our ascent up toward Saint Gotthard pass. For the first time the larger snowcapped mountains began to emerge. Each seemed to be larger and more beautiful than the last. Collectively, we could not all absorb the grandeur. Our drive carried us to heights of more than twelve thousand feet. We were wonder-struck by the splendid scenery that enveloped us.

Expressions of elation abounded. Each new landscape brought "ohs," gasps, and exclamations of exuberance. We were beholding a life-size, animated storybook.

One young lady in our party was especially appreciative of what we were seeing. Spontaneous squeals of glee were occasionally accompanied by applause. Every utterance let us know she had inherited the Alps.

The meek are not weak, and the weak are not meek.
To be weak is to be
  cowering,
    capitulating,
      compromising, and
       conforming.
To be meek is to be
  controlled,
    channeled,
      curbed,
       chaste, and
        courageous.
To inherit is to
  gain the delight,
    even without the deed.
To inherit is to
  enjoy use
    without enjoining use.
To inherit is
  an inherent right,
    not an inerrant role.
The Spirit-controlled
  do not grab up the earth;
    they inherit its true value
      from their heavenly Father.

The State

BLESSED-MAKARIOS

In Greek life the word was used to describe
  the carefree life of the gods
    who did not suffer the common
      troubles of humanity.
The Athenians used it to refer to
  the very wealthy
    who were not subject to cares and worries.
Jesus brought it down to earth.
He made it available to us. What?
What did he make available to us?
The state which he called
  Blessed,
    which means:
  "How Happy,"
  "Joyous,"
  "Fulfilled,"
  "Fortunate,"
    and
  "To Be Congratulated."
These teachings of his are called the Beatitudes.
The word is derived from the Latin *beatus,*
  which means *Blessed or Happy.*
Before us we have the character that will make one
  blessed and happy.
In a time when society was sick
  of hair-splitters, ecclesiastic rules,

ceremonies, and moral expedients,
   Christ spoke.
In a day when society is sick
  of quasi-religion, relativistic thinking,
    creeds, and the new morality,
      Christ needs to be heard.
In an hour when society is sick
  of personality cults, trend setters, and
    power blocks
      Christ still has a word for us.
        Blessed! Yes, you know, blessed.
Dig down deep in a lexicon
  or Bible dictionary.
You will find the meaning,
  "God's gift to you."
Blessed is the person who is rich.
Blessed is the person who is always right.
Blessed is the person who is popular.
Blessed is the person who is strong.
Blessed is the person who rules.
The world adds all them up and they equal success.

Blessed is the person who is charming.
Blessed is the person who is brilliant.
Blessed is the person who is witty.
Blessed is the person who is suave.
The world adds all them up and they equal success.

Blessed is the person who lives life with gusto.
Blessed is the person who is chic or slick.
Blessed is the person who is a real kick.
Blessed is the person who is cool.
The world adds all them up and they equal success.

Blessed are the poor in spirit.
Blessed are they that mourn.
Blessed are the meek.
Blessed are they which do hunger and thirst.

Blessed are the merciful.
Blessed are the pure in heart.
Blessed are the peacemakers.
Blessed are they which are persecuted.
Christ adds all them up and they equal faithfulness.

Ultimately—if anybody is interested in that,
    it will result in his
        "Well done . . . "

4
How to Satisfy an Insatiable Appetite

Self-evaluation will lead one to realize: "I am a magic kingdom!"

The wonderful world of *me* has creative power. I have numerous departments: energy, war, health, welfare, education, commerce, transportation—these are but a few.

My complexity is unexcelled by any nation on earth. There is within me a microcosm of mankind.

Physically, I am a maze of intricate components. Just one square inch of my skin is estimated to contain 20 blood vessels, 13 sensory points for cold, 78 for heat, 165 for pressure, 65 muscles, 100 glands secreting fatty matter, 650 sweat glands, 28 nerves, 1,300 nerve ends to record pain, and 19,500 sensory cells at the end of nerve fibers.

Even people who do not have a big heart do have one that is a wonder. All the blood of the body passes through the heart every half-minute. It has a grip stronger than a fist. The two ventricles of the heart hold about ten ounces of blood which they pump out with every beat. At 72 beats per minute, that is 45 pounds per minute, 2,700 pounds per hour, and 64,800 pounds per day. That is 32.4 tons per day. That is equivalent to raising its own weight 13,000 feet per hour.

My brain will boggle your mind. It weighs between forty and fifty ounces. Almost 80 percent of this is water. The remaining ten ounces of gray cells have the capacity of storing over ten trillion units of information. That is two and one-half times more information than can be stored in the most sophisticated computer. A bit of brain tissue the size of a pinhead can store as much information as most computers.

No nation's central intelligence system can compare with my central nervous system. Variety and versatility are the hallmarks of my existence. These cells are arranged in highly specialized groups for various purposes such as communication with one another (autonomic nerves), transmitting information from the outside world (sensory nerves), or precipitating the contraction of muscles (motor nerves).

These are but a few hints regarding the marvel of me. I am an awe-inspiring world.

Any organized community has to be governed. Every society has to have structure. Who, therefore, rules in the realm of me? Who is in control?

No nation can exist and prosper if its internal affairs are controlled by outside influences. Colonization is depleting.

A nation without control is controlled by anarchists. Misrule becomes the rule. An ungoverned community soon becomes a wild kingdom.

Who is in control? It does matter. No external influence can dominate me without my consent. Internal disorders are significantly influenced by me. Only as I let outside influences seep through my defenses can they control me.

My feelings, emotions, and sentiments are not determined by what happens around me as much as by my attitude. I am no man's marionette unless I will to be. My strings are mine to control. My drives and desires determine my reasoning and responses.

Jesus knew this, and he spoke of happiness as being given birth from within. We cannot blame others. We can with his help control instead of being controlled.

Hunger (peinaō) means to avidly desire something. It signifies a need for nourishment. Those who have this trait are outwardly and inwardly deficient in the things essential to life as God meant it. It is a desire, fed by a painful lack, that God's will be done.

Thirst (dipsaō) means a yearning, a passionate desire for a spiritual good without which one can't live.

An unknown sage has suggested there are nine requisites for contented living: wealth enough to support your needs; strength to battle with difficulties and overcome them; grace enough to confess your sins and forsake them; patience enough to toil until some good is accomplished; charity enough to see some good in your neighbor; love enough to move you to be useful and helpful to others; faith enough to make real the things of God; hope enough to remove all anxious fears concerning the future.

This vestige of virtue could well be summed up as a strategic segment of righteousness. Any person strongly desiring these as dominant traits in his disposition aspires to worthy goals. Most persons set their heart on some of these sometimes. To hunger and thirst after them would be to continually maintain them.

The expression "hunger and thirst" is in the present tense of the participle in the Greek. It indicates this craving is not occasional, but constant and habitual.

It is important that our desires be the best because we inevitably get what we desire. The Bible plainly states, "As [a man] he thinketh in his heart, so is he" (Prov. 23:7).

"Our life is," said Marcus Aurelius, "what our thoughts make it."

Dr. Walter Scott, president of Northwestern University, has commented, "Success in business is caused more by mental attitudes than by mental ability."

"The ideas and images in men's minds are the invisible powers that constantly govern them," mused Jonathan Edwards.

The late William James, eminent Harvard psychologist, noted, "Belief creates the actual fact."

One of America's most thought-provoking thinkers, Ralph Waldo Emerson, wrote of the importance of desires— "Thoughts rule the world."

The prominent minister William Ellery Channing professed his belief in the importance of thought power: "Secret study, silent thought, is the mightiest agent in human affairs. What a man does outwardly is but the expression and completion of his inward thought."

These great thinkers have simply rephrased the fact that we get and become what we desire. Our appetite affects our attitude and action. In reading a menu we select that for which we have a taste.

Jesus chose two basic appetites, hunger and thirst, to dramatize our drives. This is an expression that relates to all appetites, not just food.

Athletes hunger for a win. Many have an adrenal thirst for victory. Often a person who lacks a little competitive edge is spoken of as not being hungry enough. People are driven by desires, inspired by ideals, motivated by mental pictures, and challenged by concepts. Often persons who do not extend themselves for a cause are spoken of as "not having an appetite for it."

A freshman at Amherst College put a large "V" over his door the first week on campus. Many curious quips and probing questions resulted during the four years it remained there. Near the end of his senior year he was asked to deliver the valedictory address at the graduation exercise. Then, for the first time, it became perfectly clear what the "V" represented. The youth's burning ambition was fueled every time he saw it. He had a real hunger to finish first in his class.

King David spoke descriptively of a little deer thirsting for the water brook. He likened it to his desire for righteousness.

Personal ingenuity reaches a zenith when people start devising means to get their desires. Resolution results in responsive regimentation.

When Dynasty Explorations, Ltd., was organized by Ronald Markham, he had a dream. The board of directors shared his aspirations. They agreed on twenty-three target sites for drilling. Careful planning went into their selection. The first twenty-two were disasters. The board of directors were ready to clean their bits and quit. Ron's persistency prevailed. They proceeded to drill number twenty-three. It was begun as a spiritless venture because their twenty-third target site had been drilled previously by another company. Markham's company was right on the mark. When they had drilled five feet farther than the other company, they hit the largest silver/zinc ore deposit ever struck in that part of the world. It is estimated to have been worth over two billion dollars. That is enough to satisfy the most ambitious appetite.

Aspirations and ambitions, like two twists of a rope, mutually mix with each other and twine around one's will. They bind us to productive good if they are virtuous, or else gird us to grief if they are improper.

Inordinant appetites, improperly fed, can be very defeating.

Along the coast of Maine there once lived one of the largest and most strikingly beautiful flocks of sea gulls along the Eastern seaboard. They were known for their sleek, trim bodies. Their swift flight revealed well-muscled bodies. Their endless energy resulted in maneuvers that caused many to marvel. Their brilliant plumage glistened in the sun.

Each morning, they would wing their way swiftly out to sea. Their days were spent fighting the wind currents in pursuit of their prey. They were skilled fishers. Superb stamina was required by their great fishing range. Their vigorous lifestyle made this a beautiful flock of gulls.

When nature hinted to them that winter was on its way, the flock instinctively started south. Key West was for years their migratory destination. It was easy to tell when they arrived. Their energy and beauty caused them to stand out among the other birds gathered there.

A sudden Atlantic storm forced them down one winter on Conch Island, just off the coast of St. Augustine, Florida. The quieting of the storm was followed by the breaking of a beautiful new day. Their intended overnight haven was already inhabited by a large number of gulls. Instinctively, the new arrivals waited for their hosts and hostesses to guide them to their feeding grounds.

The members of the Floridian flock were better fed and fatter than they. The plump local populace was sloven in actions and sluggish in flight. Nevertheless, the northern visitors followed their listless new acquaintances to what had to be superior fishing waters.

The flight was brief. Only a few hundred yards away they found nearly one hundred fishing vessels anchored. Fishermen were involved in their customary cleaning of their nets. Dainty tidbits that had been caught in the nets were being thrown into the sea. Meaty morsels of shrimp and other delicacies were easily accessible. It was a feast requiring little effort.

Conch Island was too good to pass up. It became the new winter quarters for the northern visitors. Southern hospitality was so good that they decided to extend their visit in the spring and not return to their former home in Penobscot Bay. Their new feeding grounds gave great bonuses for little efforts. Virtually no effort was rewarded with superior dining.

Soon the two flocks merged. One morning they leisurely winged their way over to their careless cafeteria. Their sluggish flight resulted in a stunning sight. The fleet was gone. A return visit the next day consequented in the same dismay. Subsequent visits produced the same disappointment.

Residents of the area tell of their pity for the flock's virtually wingless wonders. The beaches of the area were filled with strolling, squawking sea gulls for several weeks. Pathetically, they walked the beach, squealing and screeching. Many of the formerly beautiful birds actually starved to death. They had lost their desire, drive, dynamic, ability, ambition, and strength. Built to battle the buffeting ocean winds, they were stranded on the shore, starving.

Is there a lesson? Out of antiquity, Job reminded us that the Lord said, "Ask . . . the fowls of the air, and they shall tell thee" (Job 12:7).

Inordinate Appetites

All that hunger and thirst shall be filled—even those who hunger and thirst for the wrong things, in the wrong way, and at the wrong time. Appetites have a way of being appeased.

Not all that is filling is satisfying, however. Consider four of the greatest rulers of all time.

Alexander the Great completely conquered the world of his era. He then wept because there was no more to master. In frustrated anger, he set fire to a city and died in debauchery. He greedily gorged himself, and that resulted in grief.

Hannibal had inestimable wealth. He filled three bushels with golden rings removed from slain knights. He died of poison administered by his own hand. He was buried in a foreign land unwept and unmourned. He selfishly stuffed himself, but was never satisfied.

Julius Caesar conquered more than eight hundred cities. He dyed his robes in the blood of defeated foes. In the very place he had enjoyed some of his greatest triumphs, he was slain by his closest confidant. He had feasted and yet died famished—an empty man.

Napoleon Bonaparte, the scourge of Europe, was a prideful conqueror. Empires bowed before his might. A continent cowered in the wake of his power. His enormous ego aroused his appetite for conquest. He died in exile, a banished, conquered captive. His diet of destruction left him desolate and defeated.

They were filled, but not fulfilled. Their appetites were gratified, but never satisfied. They ate sumptuously, but their hunger was never healed. They drank deeply, but their thirst was never quenched.

The absence of hunger and thirst is an indication of sickness. Often a doctor can judge the state of one's health by the appetite. Loss of appetite indicates diminishing health. Inevitably, if it is not restored, there will be a further deterioration in vigor and stamina. One must be nourished if health is to be maintained. This is an inflexible physical and spiritual law. As with dietary nourishment, so it is with the divine diet. One must be fed the right menu.

If one has lost his appetite for things of the Spirit, there is a spiritual reason. Abstinence from spiritual food is a symptom of something significant. Quacks treat symptoms; doctors treat diseases. Force-feeding never works. The cause of a loss of appetite must be diagnosed and treated. Only when it is cured will the appetite be corrected.

The holy hunger and timely thirst of which Christ spoke are the hallmark of those who desire to be right with God. Such appetites indicate spiritual vitality. Spiritually energetic people keep on hungering and thirsting. They hunger and thirst after righteousness. It is not as though they have already attained it. Like the natural appetite for food, no matter how much one eats, the appetite soon returns. The craving is as important as the filling.

No persons should ever fear to eat and drink fully because of apprehension of depleting the supply. There is plenty in the Lord's pantry. His cupboard is never bare. He is able to feed even the most rapidly growing of his children.

Jesus said, "I am the bread of life: he that cometh to me shall never hunger; and he that believeth on me shall never thirst" (John 6:35).

Appetite expresses an expedient eagerness. In the spiritual realm it reveals true growth and maturity. Longing for the lordship of Christ is as natural as physically craving basic nutrition. To curb an appetite would mean a reduction in productive potential.

Inspiring Aspirations

Righteousness is the admirable object advocated by Christ. This quality is referred to in the Greek present tense. It means continuous action. This is an attribute which is never obtained securely. It is life's quest. As the physical appetite is never secured, but constantly needs feeding, so this sprirtual pilgrimage is perpetual. Consistency is among virtues as diamonds are among jewels. It is the Cadillac of character.

Righteousness is in the accusative case, meaning literally: "Blessed are they who do hunger and thirst after righteousness" (Matt. 5:6).

Happy is the person whose most intense desire is to enter into a right relationship with God. Righteousness carries with it a sense of justification. It refers to a right relationship with God. Right living before God is an attribute which is to be earnestly desired. Right living is always right. God has never asked us to do one thing that is not for our good. Everything he tells us to do is for our welfare. All the things he forbids are restricted for our advantage. One of our founding fathers expressed it well: "Sin is not hurtful because it is forbidden. Sin is forbidden because it is hurtful." The person who desires righteousness is actually seeking that which is best for himself.

When there is a change of state, it is to be accompanied by a transformation of character. An accused criminal may be acquitted of a charge, or convicted and pardoned. He may, however, leave the courtroom with all the character of a criminal still as strong as ever within him. His condition has changed, but not his character. This principle is not true in the spiritual realm. Where there is a change of state, called justification, there is a change of character, evidenced by a change of conduct.

Sunlight is a combination of all colors. It can be diffused into the various basic colors through a prism. A rainbow does the same. Without the sunlight, no object has any color. As soon as the sun sets and its light disappears, all color vanishes from the landscape. Subtle differences of texture or superficies cause the object to absorb or diffuse various rays. Hence, color is produced. The proportions in which this is done cause different hues. Human nature is similar. When the Sun of Righteousness shines in one's life, the characteristics of his grace color all of life.

When one is justified in a court of law, he enjoys only one primary benefit of acquittal. His acquittal before the bar results only in the release from punishment. The person whom God pardons not only receives the negative benefit of not having to suffer the consequence of punishment, but the positive advantage of spiritual assets being added. It is as though his penalty has not only been paid before the tribunal; but a deposit sufficient for lifelong support has been credited to the account of the one pardoned. This produces happiness.

Righteousness is a desire to see God's will prevail over evil. It depicts a sense of seeing God's right will done and evil rejected. When this is not done, righteousness blossoms into vindication. At this stage there is a will to see right revived and evil dethroned. The person who is righteous desires the cause of righteousness to be vindicated.

A pickle can never be a cucumber again. Sand can't run uphill in an hourglass. There is no way to unscramble an egg. The heavenly Father can, however, enable old things to pass away and all things to become new in human nature. The new nature is one of righteousness. The leopard can't lose his spots; nor can the Ethiopian change the color of his skin; but God can change one's spiritual state. At times this may seem more inconceivable than the aforementioned impossibilities. Only with God are *all* things possible. Such a change removes the prefix from unrighteous. The righteous are those with a "right-wise" relationship with God.

This relationship involves both regeneration and reformation. Spiritual regeneration must be paralleled by moral reformation. They are not either/or options, but both/and obligations. The righteous are regenerated and reformed. God does not pardon a rebel who has not ended his rebellion. A case from the files of justice illustrates this.

A state governor visited his largest prison incognito. He shared with one winsome young man in his cell. Their conversation was amiable. The governor developed an almost instant liking for the prisoner. There was an openness between them. Not knowing his visitor was the governor, the young convict was very expressive. Casually, the governor asked, "What would you do if you were lucky enough to obtain a pardon?" Instantly, there was snapped back a snarled reply: "If I ever get out of this place, the first thing I'll do is cut the throat of the judge who sent me here." The idea of the pardon was dropped. The governor left, and the young man remained in prison. A pardon of one not reformed would have been unrealistic.

To hunger and thirst after righteousness simply means to

long to be positively holy. The person who has this spiritual appetite epitomizes the Beatitudes. The harvest of the Spirit is seen in actions, attitudes, and utterances. Such a person doesn't want to be known as Superman or Wonder Woman, but Scriptureman or New Testament Woman. Their bold will is to show forth Christ. The entire being of such a person is fuel for his fire.

One hungering and thirsting after righteousness has a palate to be like people who have evidenced a voracious taste for the will of God. They display a longing to be like such persons as Abraham, Daniel, Joshua, Jeremiah, Isaiah, or Moses. Such a desire is not motivated by an ambition to gain the benefits they enjoyed, but simply to share the fellowship they knew.

Balaam, the false prophet of the Old Testament, is an example of one who wanted the benefits without the belief. Balaam mused, "Let me die the death of the righteous, and let my last end be like his!" (Num. 23:10). He wanted to die like the righteous, but he did not want to live like them. The longing of those who relish righteousness is to live and die like predecessors in faith. They are willing to pay the price of admission. They are not counterfeit welfare Christians— able to work, but unwilling. Ambitiously, they avoid filing a fraudulent claim for benefits undeserved. The deposit of life in time seems little compared to the dividends of eternal life. Spiritually, this is a "no deposit-no return" life-style.

The spiritual appetite differs in a very distinct way from the physical. In the spiritual realm the process of hungering and thirsting is a continuing process. Strangely, so is the activity of being filled. Physically, hungering and thirsting and being filled are counterproductive. Not so spiritually. Those who hunger and thirst most are filled most. Those most filled hunger and thirst most. The craving increases the capacity, and the capacity increases the craving. Each feeds and fuels the other. It is not that they are unsatisfied, just unsatiated.

There is an active element in both appetite and its appeasement. People who earnestly desire something are seldom passive about it. They become activists in pursuing it. Aggressively, they seek to acquire it. This applies in this matter also.

There is no law of diminishing return regarding righteousness. In the physical realm, values diminish with an increase of goods. One ice cream cone is superbly delicious. Two are delicious. Three are good, four OK. Five are sickening. Six would be repulsive. Spiritual appetites do not work in this regard. Consumption increases capacity. Righteousness itself is an appetite stimulant. The more one is like the Master, the more he will like the Master. The more one likes the Master, the more he will desire to be like the Master. The two form an ascending, ever enlarging spiral. Righteousness moves upward and outward: upward to the eternal ideal, Jesus Christ, and outward toward humanity in his name.

Certain constructive actions need to be taken to assure an ambitious appetite. It can be curbed only by carnality. Therefore, always observe basic dietary laws.

Always avoid appetite suppressants. Stay away from those things that are contrary to righteousness. We cannot make ourselves righteous. We can, by our own initiative, avoid eating from life's gutters. A nauseated person cannot enjoy even the most savory foods. There are certain things that are instinctively and biblically known to be in conflict with righteousness. Don't taste them. To avoid the temptation to do so, don't even sniff their aroma. Physically, if you know a certain food makes you sick, you shouldn't eat it. The same is true spiritually.

Avoid things that dull your appetite. There are some that are not bad in themselves; however, some persons have an allergy to them. It is not only wise, but basic that persons should avoid those things to which they know they are allergic. In the spiritual menu there are also some things that are not bad in themselves; but neither are they always good for persons. Any individual should know his own appetite and system. Avoid an allergy-causing diet. Every person has that which is referred to as that "sin which doth so easily beset us" (Heb. 12:1). Avoid it.

Seek spiritual appetite stimulants. Good friends who share
your appetite for righteousness are an asset. Systematic Bible
study, a daily refreshing prayer life, sharing one's faith, and
a wholesome social calendar increase one's appetite. Public
worship is a vital stimulus to righteousness.

Inspiring Assurances

Filled comes from a passive Greek verb. It indicates that
God does the filling. The individual can and should avail self
of such, but only God can do it. The sufficiency of the filling
is indicated by the basic meaning of the word. It does not
just indicate that the appetite will be appeased. It indicates
that the person will be made fat. This means a spiritual energy
reserve. It pictures contentment and satisfaction. When God
fills, he stuffs and gorges.

Respectfully, Matthew omitted God's name in the Beatitudes by using the passive voice. The happiness of which
they speak is shown by the passive voice to come only from
God. Seeking happiness at other fountains is like trying to
take a pill at a water cooler. It just doesn't go down right.
Counterfeit sources of happiness are fountains flowing with
salt water and cupboards infected with botulism. They tempo-
rarily satisfy, but ultimately sicken.

Dr. Peter Rossi, a sociologist at the University of Chicago,
observed, "All it takes to be happy is youth, money, success,
good health, and a wife. Possessing these requisites, one has
found a wellspring of happiness." All of these are laudable.
Any person would approve of each as a valued quality. However, they make happiness for the elderly, poor, unsuccessful,
sickly and females unlikely. There are no such restrictions
in God's provisions. Conversely, sometimes some of the most
miserable persons have all of these assets. King Solomon once
was a living embodiment of all these and other materialistic
assets. Summarily, he said, "I hated life . . . for all is vanity
and vexation of spirit" (Eccl. 2:17).

Vanity, as he used it, is a term that depicts a vacuum. Solomon concluded that trying to find happiness apart from the

righteousness of God is like filling a vacuum with a vacuum. It does not fill with anything of substance. It only produces more emptiness.

Vexation of spirit is also a graphic. Solomon's experience demonstrated a basic truth. Trying to find true and lasting happiness apart from the righteousness of God is like feeding the appetite for physical food by inhaling the aroma. It is like feeding on wind. No matter how big the banquet table nor how savory its scent, one can never be filled if all he does is inhale. Inhalation and appetite are not related. There is no way one can satisfy the other. Inhalation can tease, but it can never please appetite.

Nero, emperor of the mighty Roman Empire, abounded in the pleasures of the world and was not satisfied. He had wealth. His crown was valued at more than a half-million dollars, before inflation. A thousand chariots accompanied him on all trips. He never wore the same garment twice. He became so fatigued by passing pleasures that he offered a bonus to anyone who devised new ones. He lived a miserable, peevish, gloomy life. He died a lonely death by suicide. He had the capacity to sip from every source of counterfeit happiness. None satisfied.

Shortly before his death, the reclusive Howard Hughes was asked if he was happy. The reply of the world's richest man was, "No, not really."

These are but three examples of persons who tried wisdom, works, wealth, wine, and women and found the cherished chalice to contain worms. God alone fills. He fills only the seekers of righteousness.

Actor Zero Mostel perhaps spoke more wisdom than he realized when asked about the secret of happiness. He responded, "Getting lost—being involved in something you can't understand. Mystery is the main thing in life. Why should you have to understand everything?"

The mystery of righteousness is a challenge with meaning. It is fulfilling. Its by-product is happiness as promised in the seminar on the summit of Mount Beatitudes. The source is still exclusively the same. Logic and experience make this understandable, though it can never be understood. By getting lost in an attempt to fill one's spiritual appetite, one finds a peculiar filling. It is refreshing. It renews. It is righteousness. One does not have to understand it to experience it and enjoy its benefit—happiness.

> This unmitigated joy,
>   unlimited happiness,
>   unexcelled blessing
> resulting from righteousness
>   (regeneration and reformation)
> has a single source,
>   is available to selective souls,
>   and is of a sufficient supply.
> To seek it
>   as an end in itself
>   is to find a life
>   filled
>   full of meaning
>   because it is
>   FULFILLING.
> It is not available to those who seek the end,
>   happiness,
>   without the means,
>   righteousness.

The Source

THE SOURCE

Earthly treasures,
  food and raiment,
    houses and land,
      abundance of material goods—
These were the things on the minds
    of the persons Christ addressed.
Money and merchandise,
  property and securities,
    fortune and opulence,
      riches and plenty
  were shown to be
    no foundation
      on which to establish
        a pleasant and productive life.
"A man's life consisteth not
  in the abundance
    of the things
      which he possesses."
The person blessed is the one who
  has within his heart
The treasures of
  patience and peaceableness,
    purity and meekness,
      a heart tender toward people,
        love for God.

This fulfilled life can never come
  from an empty heart,
    Regardless of how full
      one's purse may be.

BE A PART OR APART

Jesus began to teach them
  What he taught was intended to tear.
He intended it to tear away
  the foolish illusions
    of the multitude
      regarding the nature of the Kingdom.
  And it did.
    What he said
      forms a set of paradoxes
        to the fleshly mind.
  And it did.
Jesus dashed water
  on their fiery, impure enthusiasm.
One greater than Gideon
  was testing his troops.
Persons interested in happiness
  apart from the Person
    are hapless.
As those interested in
  a kingdom of gross delights
    and vulgar conquests
      turned back
You who want
  happiness apart from the one who produces it
Stop reading.

5
How to Be Understood

Eudaemonics is defined by Webster as the science of happiness. *Eudaemonism* is said to be the system of ethics which holds that the bases of moral obligations lie in their relation to the production of happiness. The most distinctly distilled system of ethics ever proposed was expounded by Christ. The Beatitudes deal precisely with happiness. The definition of eudaemonics implies that there are certain scientific principles involved in happiness. Science is a study dealing with a body of facts or truths systematically arranged and showing the operation of general laws. Christ did systematize certain basic principles essential to happiness. These truths are eudaemonics at its best. They constitute a simple succinct system of thought, which if practiced produces a certain result—happiness. Various laws of chemistry and mathematics are fixed. Their inflexibility has been demonstrated for generations. Likewise, the beautiful attitudes spoken of by Christ are just as demonstrable and fixed. They work.

One can struggle against the basic mathematical principle that two plus two equals four, but it does inevitably add up every time. Certain components result in concrete conclusions. Protest or pretense will not keep the total of two and two from equaling four. The involvement of the eight insights shared by Christ are just as certain to equal the same total every time. It is happiness.

The heavenly Father said, "I will put my law in their inward parts, and write it in their hearts" (Jer. 31:33). His covenant is an inward one. It is made between God and the person in the inner person. Thereafter, there is an intimate under-

standing in the innermost rooms of our being. This refreshing
intimacy has various stages. First, his law was written in the
Bible. At this stage the law is still entirely outside the person.
Since it is external, there may be no internal influence on
one's life. Secondly, the law may be embedded in the mind.
At this point of memorization it becomes a thought. It may
become an ambition and aspiration that controls much of
life. Thirdly, the law may enter into the heart. At this juncture
it becomes an affection that affects the disposition. It abides
as an inmate in the room of reason and response. These three
planes of endearment and involvement form an ascending
gradient of intimacy. The ultimate elevation is most desirable.
The will of the Father is not just expressed in the Bible or
upon the level of thought; but it becomes an ambitious affection. Upon reading his word, we are to discern his will by
our mind and do his work from our heart. Then the laws of
happiness add up. What they promise, they produce.

Florence Nightingale's image emerges when one thinks of
mercy. She represents God's law on the third plane. She wrote
in her diary at Cairo, "Oh God, thou puttest into my heart
this great desire to devote myself to the sick and sorrowful.
I offer it to thee. Do with it what is for thy service." What
had been put in her heart prompted her to write of herself,
"Behold the handmaid of the Lord!" She found and fulfilled
her calling. In mercy she ministered to many.

Humanity has long been engaged in the search for happiness. Knowing human nature, Christ addressed this ceaseless
craving. His summit symposium by the sea gave attention
to the subject. Eight inspiring ideals are shared that collectively produce happiness. They refer to eight aspects of one
life, not a diverse group of people each having one.

"Happiness is purely internal," says psychologist Dr. Matthew N. Chappell. "It is produced not by objects, but by ideals,
thoughts and attitudes which can be developed and constructed by the individual's own activities, irrespective of the
environment."

Christ was more concerned about the disposition of his

followers than about their dealings. The truths he taught place the primary emphasis upon being rather than doing. His teaching involves the core of our being. A superficial veneer or colorful coating is no substitute for what he demands at the center of our personality. A Christian must first *be* something before he can *do* anything. What we *are* is the basis of our action. One can occasionally act right without being right, but one cannot be right without consistently acting right. It is out of the heart that the issues of life emerge. Therefore, Christ's cornerstone teaching unveiled in Galilee deals with the temperament rather than temptation. Either can control the other. Hence, Christ sought to fortress the will against external attacks.

In his preface to *Man and Superman,* George Bernard Shaw spoke ambiguously about facts he never saw flower:

> This is the true joy in life, the being used for a purpose recognized by yourself as a mighty one; the being thoroughly worn out before you are thrown on the scrap heap; the being a force of Nature instead of a feverish, selfish little clod of ailments and grievances complaining that the world will not devote itself to making you happy.

The Beatitudes are built on the presupposition that the world does not owe you happiness; nor can it grant it. Happiness must come from within. The force is the source. The source is within. The super structure for supreme happiness is inside the individual. It is not contingent upon circumstances. If you are to be happy it must be because you are happy.

Centuries ago the sage Epictetus said, "Men are disturbed not by the things that happen, but by their opinion of the things that happen."

"The habit of being happy," observed Robert Louis Stevenson, "enables one to be freed from the domination of outward conditions."

If you resolve to wait until conditions around you are conducive for happiness, don't plan to hold your breath. The Latin word for happiness, *fortuous,* carries with it the idea of fortune. It implies that happiness is dependent on having good fortune. The word in the Greek text speaks of a joyous happiness not dependent on externals.

Gladstone wisely suggested, "Be happy with what you have and are, be generous with both, and you won't have to hunt for happiness."

"Very little is needed to make a happy life," mused Marcus Aurelius, emperor of Rome. "It is all within yourself, in your way of thinking."

Such men of wisdom only serve as footnotes to Christ's teachings regarding happiness.

Merciful (eleēmōn) means sympathy manifested in action— the emotion aroused by contact with an affliction which comes undeservedly on some other person.

The Active Attitude

Mercy is an emotion that leads to action. It is an empathetic expression of love toward those who are broken, battered, bruised, and bleeding in life's battle. Pity may move one to a show of tears, but mercy motivates action. Mercy is creative, constructive compassion. It is not just domiciled in the heart; it is demonstrated by the hands. The practical result of mercy is concern that causes involvement. When it is manifested, it unites us with God. When it is suppressed, it screens us from him. It should be expressed, not repressed.

Mercy prompts persons to be sensitive to the needs of others. This happens not because of the virtue or vantage point of others, but because of the new nature of the believer. It is an attribute that our heavenly Father has shown us. We are encouraged to "Be ye therefore merciful, as your Father also is merciful" (Luke 6:36). This is displayed discipleship on duty.

Muscle, not mercy, is the admired quality of our honor. The ability to seize, acquire, hold, secure, force, control, and mandate is applauded. Might, not right, is cherished. "Run over the rundown" and you are somebody. Assert yourself, pull your own strings, be aggressive, do your own thing, and people will sense that you are a citizen of this century.

Friedrich Wilhelm spoke of the emotions of many when he said, "Assert yourself. Care for nothing except for yourself. The only vice is weakness, and the only virtue is strength. Be strong, be superman. The world is yours if you can get it." Through Nietzsche the cult of self-expression was forcefully expressive. He died in a madhouse. The segment of the world that followed his philosophy went to the brink of hell in World War I. Darwinism was the pseudoscientific expression of this school of thought. It has been made the vogue in humanism.

In a period of history even more muscle-bound than ours, when brutality and brazenness abounded, Christ spoke of happiness coming from being merciful. It works because it worked.

Having just finished a statement on filling, Christ next moved to one regarding overflowing. The believer is to be his unclogged channel of mercy.

This is the most appealing Beatitude. Everybody loves the good Samaritan. Acts of mercy have through the centuries made well-known heroes and heroines of unknowns. As the recipients of mercy, we are all made to feel better.

This statement is strategically located in the string of inspiring insights. The first four relate to the initial attitudes of one controlled by the Spirit. The last four deal with productivity of such a life. This one indicates the first evidence and effect of a life filled and overflowing. As recipients of mercy, we become ambitious to share it. The initial ones describe attitudes essential to receiving God's designated blessings. The second segment describes the attributes of those who have made such blessings their goal.

Mercy is like a cipher in arithmetic. It may not be worth much in itself, but it is capable of adding a great deal to the value of everything else. It springs from the heart. Like an air-cushion, there may not appear to be anything in it, but it eases jolts marvelously. Mercy is no compromise of dignity. When a person is right, he can afford to be merciful. When he is wrong, he must be.

Mercy prompts one to overlook a friend's broken fence that needs painting and appreciate the roses that bloom in his garden. It is the capacity of finding a diamond in a pigpen and the ability to appreciate an orchid in a trash can. Mercy moves people to be courteous, considerate, and compassionate.

The Attainable Asset

They shall receive mercy. This virtue, like all others, is its own reward. It is a boomerang of blessing. If we show it, we shall receive it. That needs careful examination. One does not give to get. The natural consequence of showing mercy is that God gives us the greater capacity to receive for showing it. We keep getting a supply as long as we keep delivering. If this implied that we would receive mercy from others as a reward for giving it, this statement would be inaccurate. If such were the case, Christ would have said, "Blessed are the merciful, for they shall receive justice." There is no justice in mercy. The two terms cancel each other out.

This does not mean that if you are kind to others, they will be kind to you. That simply does not work. That would be manipulation of others, and each individual has a personal will which will not always respond to allow it. We train ourselves to mercy by being merciful. The self-discipline that produces mercy soon becomes second nature. The song is to the singer, and comes back most to him; the gift is to the giver, and comes back most to him; the mercy is to the merciful, and comes back most to him; it is inevitable.

Napoleon was moved by a mother's plea for a pardon on behalf of her son. However, the emperor said it was the second offense; and justice demanded death. "I do not ask for justice," implored the mother; "I plead for mercy."

"But," said the emperor, "he does not deserve mercy."

"Sire," cried the mother, "it would not be mercy if he deserved it, and mercy is all I ask for."

The compassion and clarity of logic prompted Napoleon

to respond, "Well, then, I will have mercy." The pardon was granted on the basis of mercy, not justice.

The merciful receive mercy because of God's mercy, not because of their virtue. If they earned, merited, or deserved it, then they would receive justice in return for their mercy. Mercy is God's nature. Those who have his nature show it. An unmerciful Christian is a contradiction in terms. Our mercy toward others simply indicates we have received mercy from the Father. Such an undemonstrative display of mercy enables persons to understand our new nature. It indicates we know mercy experientially.

The merciful are not naive. They kindly judge wrongdoers, but do not mistake wrongdoing. They are not blind to improper conduct. Mercy is not pity or sympathy divorced from sound judgment and moral integrity. It also goes beyond simply having a lenient attitude toward persons who have done wrong. It results in an attempt to restore such a person to a right state. Mercy is never passive. It is among the most aggressive of attitudes.

Mercy is an emotion that means feeling along with another. It is compassion at its best. It always leads to action. There has never been an act of undemonstrative mercy. There is no smattering of selfishness in it. It always has the other person's welfare at heart. It is like a spiritual transfiguration in that one's assets and abilities are available to be transferred to another in need.

Dante said of Beatrice, "Whenever she appeared before me I had no enemy left on earth; the flame of charity kindled within me and caused me to forgive all whoever had offended me." This spirit is activated in those who have received God's mercy. To reflectively enter into his presence in prayer is to come forth with mercy to all. Fellowship with God is reality and not delusion. It has a profound influence. When we share the heart of the Father, we pass his spirit on because of our joy in receiving his mercy. "Blessed be God, even the Father of our Lord Jesus Christ, the Father of mercies and the God of all comfort" (2 Cor. 1:3).

The old Greeks, whose civilization developed classic archi-

tecture, magnificent paintings, and decorative arts, said, "God
is beauty."

The Romans were led by the caesars on hundreds of battle-
fields of conquest. They boasted that the Roman eagles never
turned backward. They said, "God is might." The Jewish heri-
tage in the law of Moses prompted them to say, "God is
law." It remained for Jesus Christ to reveal that "God is merciful." His mercy is from everlasting. It has always been a characteristic of the Father. It must be a manifestation in his children.

Lady Astor visited the United States at the time when Franklin Roosevelt was elected to succeed Herbert Hoover. She
addressed a meeting in her native state of Virginia on the
state of politics in England. In the course of her address,
she stated, "The longer I am in public life, the less I care
about speaking, for it is what you are and what you do that
is important and not what you claim you are or say you are
going to do." Currently, the disillusioned, depressed, and
defeated do not want to hear our pious pronouncements.
They care not about our degree of pedigree. What they do
comprehend is our scars won in the battle of mercy on their
behalf.

Not only is it true that those who share and show mercy
are perpetual channels of mercy; but the opposite is a reality.
People who do not have mercy do not lose their souls, but
they do lose soul. There is a vibrant quality missing from
the life of those who obstinately refuse to give of themselves.
Vitality is drained when there is no compassionate expression
of concern for others. The soul of the person looks like a
jack-o'-lantern in which someone has blown out the candle.
It is dark and void of expression. There is no glow. Mercy
illuminates a life and lights the area for others.

The Alternate Action

Alternatives to mercy are available. One can vent hate toward others. In doing so, remember this couplet: "Hate does
more harm to the vessel in which it is stored than to the
one on which it is poured."

When hatred is manifested toward a person, it indicates that the person harboring the hate is mastered by another. The person hated is actually controlling the temperament of the one with hatred. His mood is actually dictated by the object of his hostility.

I visited a lady in the hospital who told me how she had hated me for eight years. Vividly, she expressed her bitterness toward me. After listening to the details, I attempted in great love to explain to her that the event which caused her hate never even happened. The logic of the explanation melted her heart in tears and reconciliation resulted. She had harbored hatred for eight years. It had kept her from attending any church. She cut herself off from the Christian community because of her hatred for a person who did not even know her and over an event that never happened. The reason for her hospitalization was a stroke caused by resentment. Mercy would have been a far better medicine.

"My soul is too glad," said Martin Luther, "and too great to be at heart the enemy of any man."

Booker T. Washington, a man often discriminated against, commented, "I . . . resolved that I would permit no man . . . to narrow and degrade my soul by making me hate him."

When the mind is filled with mercy, there is no room for hatred. Flood your mind with things that are beautiful and true, and there will be no place for animosity. Mercy melts hate as though it were fetters of ice.

Revenge is another option to mercy. Frequently it is said, "He's got it coming, and . . . " "One of these days I'm going to . . . " "She deserves . . . and I'm going to give it to her." "They are entitled to a piece of my mind and . . . " These expressions indicate that a person has done something wrong. This improper conduct, by the world's standard, deserves repayment. They have injured someone and deserve punishment. Justice would help an avenger mount up and put a lance in the hand. Vengeance would cheer on the champion. Mercy pleads for loving patience and understanding.

Persons sworn to vengeance are preoccupied with methods

of repayment and timing. Constructive creativity capitulates and becomes cunning conniving. Time and energy lose their positive outlook and are subverted by a predisposition toward "paying back."

Revenge has a backward look. No one ever progressed properly by looking backward. A resolve to rectify a wrong can ruin reason and rationality. "I'll get even with you if it takes the rest of my life . . . " has occasionally done just that: "taken" the rest of the life. That is a big price to pay. Mercy is a much more meaningful approach.

Jesus placed the responsibility for mercy on the injured party. It is only possible when one has authority and power to exact punishment. When we have been offended, the wrong should be recognized as an opportunity, not an offense. It is a moment to slay spite. By our not nourishing revenge, the spirit of Christ can be demonstrated in mercy.

Instead of seeking retribution, the merciful manifest tolerance, forgiveness, helpfulness, and encouragement. These are aggressive, continual acts. Mercy is never passive. It is productive as a result of being persistent.

Violence is another alternative to mercy. It is the older brother of hate. An instinct toward violence has seeped into our national bloodstream. Violence is not only here; it is loved. The violence syndrome of our culture has developed into a cool, guiltless method of solving problems by disposing of the people who cause them. It is triggered by hatred. Violence stirs more hatred and vicious responses. Hostility begets hostility. The cycle grows ever wider. Violence never resolves violence. Only mercy can break the chain of events.

The old code of Hammurabi, "an eye for an eye," has new devotees. Mercy says to relinquish your right to retaliation, revenge, and repayment. "But they are my rights," many assert. Mercy seeks not rights, but the right. Not one eye has ever been restored by plucking out another. Hate has never destroyed violence. Muscling and maneuvering are no match for mercy.

Mercy says, "What I care about is *you,* friend." It enables one to take an insult without resentment, to forget as well as forgive, and to pass up your right to strike back without regretting it. Interpersonal relations are put above personal rights when mercy prevails.

Three proponents of violence have hung out their laundry on history's line for all to see.

Chairman Mao Tse-tung wrote, "Political power comes out of the barrel of a gun."

Adolf Hitler declared, "I cannot see why man should not be just as cruel as nature."

Karl Marx referred to mercy as "the parson's mode of thought."

The product of their philosophy is despair, desolation, and death.

Individually and nationally, our Achilles heel may be our tolerance for violence. It is now being spoken of as normal. The danger is that what is considered "normal" soon becomes "necessary" and then "legitimate." Our species' term in office may soon be ended if mercy does not succeed in getting the foot of violence off the accelerator of self-destruction.

Bitterness, a wet nurse to violence, is another alternative to mercy. It is a poor substitute, for it paralyzes emotions, logic, reason, and responses. It may be maintained under the guise of avoiding being hurt again. It is used as a perpetual plaster cast intended to protect the wearer from further injury. It also makes rigid and weak emotions, sentiments, and feelings.

Bitterness toward individuals, as well as toward God, must be avoided.

General William Booth, esteemed founder of the Salvation Army, was dramatically stricken blind. His son, Bramwell, was given the responsibility of informing his dad there would be no recovery.

"Do you mean that I am blind?" the general queried.

"I fear we must contemplate that," was the reply.

"I shall never see your face again?"

"No, probably not in this world."

"Bramwell," responded the general, "I have done what I could for God and for the people with my eyes. Now I shall do what I can for God and for the people without my eyes." Bitterness had been banished.

Mercy keeps no score on wrongs. It will not allow a long-standing resentment or tolerate a refusal to be reconciled. It never hangs over life a "Private—Keep Out" sign in order to punish anyone with frozen friendship. One hundred and eighty degrees is never too far to turn for reconciliation.

The Admirable Aspiration

Biblically, mercy means more than letting an offender off without punishment. It seeks to restore and refurbish. Like two streams which unite their separate waters to form a common river, forgiveness and restoration flow into the tributary of mercy. As the wings of the two cherubim met above the ark, forgiveness and restoration embrace in mercy. In the ancient Jewish community, mercy involved forgiveness and almsgiving. Thus, it was twofold. It dealt with the negative by eradicating the wrong. It responded positively by aggressively seeking charitably to assist the offending party. The offended became the one energetically seeking to establish a right relationship.

The Latin for *mercy* stresses pain of heart. Compassion, feeling with, prompts one to read the heart of another. Desire moves the merciful to seek to aid other's attitude, opinion, and outlook. As a result of feeling along with the other person, concern is aroused and compassion reaches out. Mercy leads to action. The good Samaritan "showed mercy" (Luke 10:37).

In Christ's attitude-adjustment clinic by the sea, this teaching stands out as the "Red Cross Beatitude." It prompts one to seek to serve the needy, even the wealthy-needy; the hungry, even the fat-hungry; the defeated, even the victorious-defeated. The merciful sees the world as full of empty cups and seeks to fill them with cool water. There is manifested a servant spirit.

Mercy moves one's morals out of the jungle. It prompts

people to care for the weak and suffering instead of carrying them into the forest to die. It is the condition of the heart of the caring person that prompts mercy, not environment or involvement. The person moved to act is moved from within because it is his nature.

Mercy motivates and moves.
It never manipulates or manhandles.
Mercy is an attitude
    resulting in action.
It is a
    show-and-tell
        demonstration of love.
Mercy is not something you are surprised
    to find a person has.
It is evident.
Those who are merciful are not
    gullible or naive.
They are not only rational and reasoning,
    but responsible and responding.
Mercy never looks the other way.
Mercy is neither hardheaded nor hard of hearing.
Mercy wears no blinders.
When mercy knows, mercy shows.
Mercy cares,
    never despairs,
        always shares—
            has no flairs.

The Sphere

WHERE IS THE KINGDOM?

Gratified desires
  do not necessarily mean
    satisfied selves.
Platonists were not satisfied
  by their aristocratic virtue.
Epicureans were not satisfied
  by their pleasure-seeking.
Humanists are not satisfied
  by their self-elevation.
Romantics are not satisfied
  by their fantasies.
Futurologists will not be satisfied
  by their conquests.
Christ's teaching transcends
  all human thought.
He offers
  hope, glad tidings, and confidence
    to all who look to him for abundant life,
      life with superabundant additives
        inherent within it.
The Kingdom is within you.

INTERNAL ETERNALS

The Beatitudes are just
  facets, states, modes,
    and aspects of a character.
Our blessedness is within us.
It is not dependent upon our position,
  but our disposition.
It is not dependent upon our ability,
  but our availability.
It is not dependent upon our impression,
  but our expression.
It is not dependent upon our union,
  but our communion.
Our blessedness is
  within us.
How silly of us to have overlooked it.
That is where we were told it was.
"The Kingdom of heaven is within you."
Long live the King!
  And of his rule
    may there be no end.

6
How to Fulfill Your Deepest Longing

One's highest good is a pure heart. Our deepest longing is to see God. This beatific vision is realized by the pure in heart.

Our current national preoccupation with happiness is nothing new. Our Founding Fathers even included a comment regarding it in our Declaration of Independence—"We hold these truths to be self-evident, that all men are . . . endowed by their Creator with certain unalienable Rights, that among these are Life, Liberty and the pursuit of Happiness."

This passion for happiness has even driven some to demand that the government pay for the trip. The "pursuit of happiness" is understood by them to mean a license to grab more power, money, and physical pleasure. To find happiness we must not be overly concerned with what the world owes us, but what we owe the world. Our inordinate self-love has resulted in a denial of responsibility and a demand for our rights. "Unalienable right" is good theory, but impossible practice. There is no such thing. We are responsible for our happiness. It is contingent upon where and how we pursue happiness. Our probe has been in outer space, whereas the biblical counsel regards the inner place—the heart.

The mysterious aspect of happiness is that those who seek it as such never find it. It is not a destination—not an end in itself. It is written on the scroll of the heart in the ink of attitude.

Masterful means of manipulation have been devised in attempting to synthetically produce happiness, such as therapy, drugs, hyperactivity, and now a mental pacemaker. This little element is planted in the brain. It stimulates reactions by electric impulse. Early experiments involved an ape. He was made to grin 500,000 successive times by electric impulse. Weariness and fatigue were overcome by this stimuli, and a half-million grins resulted. External reaction was programmed as desired. One can't help but wonder about the stress produced by actions and emotions not in harmony. A similar stress is produced in the lives of persons acting out known desires of peers without putting their hearts in it.

It is not easy to find happiness in ourselves, but it is not possible to find it elsewhere. As far back as the Greek philosophers, we have been told that a person can only be happy as the heart allows. Happiness must reside and preside in the sanctum sanctorum of our very existence, the heart. In every person's life, it is a supreme court that passes judgment on events. Many have sought to find happiness while denying the mandates of this tribunal. Attitudes and actions, not sanctioned thereby, carry within themselves the virus of their own demise.

Many physical evidences exist that indicate that happiness is eluding most. Annually, Americans consume 7,500,000,000 sleeping pills. Happy people can surely sleep better than that. Each night 19,000,000 shaky hands reach for help. Eleven million pounds of aspirin are consumed per year. Someone has calculated that represents about 7,500,000,000 headaches, or fifty headaches per head per year. Physical reasons may account for many of those. Fatigue in the pursuit of happiness doubtless accounts for many.

Happiness consists in what you are, not what you have. Anatole France told of a fabled king who sought happiness. He was informed that he would be cured of his illness and made happy if he would wear the shirt of a happy man. Emissaries of the king were ordered to search for a happy man. They chanced to meet a little man who lived in a hollow plane tree in the forest. His name was Mousque. His unhandsome face was always lit with a smile. Laughter often uncovered his square teeth. He lived on the forest and from the lake, and apparently lived well. His unattractiveness was often overlooked because he knew how to please people and make himself useful. He worked harder and longer than others. Greater joy was found in fatigue than seemed normal. He lived to serve.

Members of the king's party often heard villagers refer to being "happy as Mousque." This proverb impressed the seekers. One day they found him playing with a puppy. He was apparently as happy as the puppy. They asked whether he was happy.

Mousque could not answer. He had never reflected on the subject. They explained the meaning of the word. After a brief moment of contemplation, he answered that he possessed it. Upon hearing this reply, one of the king's men cried out, "Mousque, we will get you everything you want— gold, a palace, new shoes, anything that you would like— but give us your shirt."

His kind face expressed neither disappointment nor regret, but great surprise. He made a sign that he could not give them what they asked of him. He did not own a shirt.

To be as "happy as Mousque," we must be of a similar disposition. Happiness must be self-contained, but supremely maintained. Its origin is God. Its source is self. Happiness is theo-factured (fashioned by God's hands), not manufactured.

Pure (katharos) means being cleansed, free from soil or stain; not double-minded with a divided heart; free of hypocrisies and falsehoods; morally free from stain or shame; free of adulteration. Full and unreserved self-offering to God rules out anything which is not of God.

Requirement

This sixth Beatitude tells of our highest possibility and our deepest longing. The possibility is a pure heart, and the longing is to see God.

There was then, as now, no need to urge persons simply to change their life-styles. Exhortations to cease stealing, committing adultery, cohabiting, deceiving, and surrendering to temptation do little good. One's nature must be changed.

If there is bacteria in a culture, it will grow. If there is yeast in dough, it will multiply. If there is contamination in the heart, it will develop and defile the whole life.

Jesus addressed these words initially to persons who were concerned with purity. They were interested in ancestral, dietary, hygienic, and ceremonial purity. Our culture is no less interested in purity. We have pure food and drug laws. The need for water and air have sent people to the streets with placards. We demand pure oil for our cars, pure food for our pets, and pure sweeteners for out tables. Christ was concerned for the most important purity of all—purity of heart.

Utter sincerity or single-mindness is the reference. It is the opposite of hypocrisy. In the Greek theater the word translated *hypocrite* was used to describe a play actor. An actor might appear on stage wearing one costume and a certain mask. Later the same actor might appear wearing a different costume, another mask, and elevator shoes to play another role. Such role players were called hypocrites. They were two-faced, not sincere, and only playacting. This is the opposite of what is urged by the expression "pure in heart."

Impurity of life is a great heresy. It is a travesty against one's best self. We each would do well to cry out with the psalmist, "Create in me a clean heart, O God" (Ps. 51:10).

George Washington wrote his friend Governor Morris, who was about to visit Europe. He requested him "to buy me in Paris a flat gold watch; not the watch of a fool or of a man desirous to make a show, but of which the interior construction shall be extremely well cared for, and the exterior very simple." That is precisely what is personified in a person of a pure heart. There is no brassy, brazen display produced from an empty heart.

Purity is the *fons et origo* of every attitude and action.

The Greek word *katharos* had broad secular use. It was used to describe an army purged of all disloyal discontent and cowardly soldiers. Gideon's remnant would have been spoken of as pure. Milk or wine unadulterated with water was declared pure. In reference to persons, it means one whose motives are always entirely unmixed.

This enables a person to be free from the tyranny of a divided self, trying to serve God and the world. No man can serve two masters. Such an attempt results in a moral conflict that is self-destructive. "Purify your hearts," said James, the son of Mary and Joseph, "ye double-minded" (Jas. 4:8).

Dr. Sladen of the Ford Hospital in Detroit supervised 140 doctors. Addressing his medical colleagues, he stated, "Gentlemen, in medicine you and I need in a day like this, when men are cracking up all around us, something more than you can buy in the corner pharmacies; we need a great grip on God." He explained how he and nine other doctors were commissioned by the United States government to draw up a list of ten laws of public health. They reduced the number from ten to nine. Their foundation was the Beatitudes of Christ. In each instance they changed the word from *blessed* to *healthy*. Thus their list was compiled: "Healthy are the pure in heart . . ."

When a life is purged of impurity, it has unmixed devotion and unadulterated motives. That which begins as a divided mind develops into a disturbed mind and deteriorates into a distressed mind. This pulling apart within a person's conscience fractures personality and shivers sensibility. It is nerve-racking.

For this and other reasons, Christ pleads for a pure heart—that is, one with undivided affections, open simplicity, and sincere genuineness. It is not enough to be clean outwardly. Inward purity is the mandate. This involves purity of desires, motives, interest, and intent. Every person should ask, "Are my motives pure? Are my intentions genuine?"

Purity of heart may apply to being free of deception and clean of defilement. The process of cleansing often requires time. It must be accomplished by a divine agent—Jesus Christ.

In Atlanta, Georgia, there stands the massive Henry W. Grady Memorial Hospital. The man whose name it bears was a leader of the New South after the Civil War. He was an editor and an eloquent speaker. While attending the International Convention of the YMCA in Atlanta, he was moved by their closing ceremony. Grady refused to clasp hands with others and sing the closing hymn. Later he said that the young men who did so had something which was lacking in his life. He recalled how years before, at his home in Athens with his beloved mother, he had had it. It had been contaminated by circumstances and conditions. He acknowledged a desire to once again experience such a wholesome, clean feeling. One young man shared with him what Jesus had done to cleanse his life. This stirred a stronger interest in the statesman.

The following day this famous Southerner checked out of his office. He informed friends that he would be gone for a week. He caught the first train back to the home of his childhood. A reversion that revitalized his life occurred. He asked his mother to treat him just as she had when he was a boy. Pie-dough cakes, apple turnovers, and ginger horses with raisin eyes followed. In the quiet afternoons, he would recline on the couch and ask his mother to retell the stories of his youth. He requested such narratives as Joseph and his many-colored coat, David and his sling, and Daniel and the lions.

Often he would bring the Bible to the table and ask her to read the sweet story of the birth of Jesus. He requested her to read about Jesus' life of service, suffering, and death.

When he went to bed at night, he requested his mother to hear his prayers. Then once again he would pray as many giants before him: "Now I lay me down to sleep. I pray the Lord my soul to keep." Grady stayed for two weeks in his boyhood home with his mother. He emerged a new and renewed man. Something had happened in his life. His spirit, mind, and body were cleansed and refreshed.

Upon returning to Atlanta, he found an invitation on his desk. The New England Society of New York City had requested him to be their featured speaker at their annual meeting.

At the dinner he was seated next to General Sherman. His buoyant spirit was free of bitterness toward the man who had burned Atlanta. He observed that Mr. Sherman was a fine man, "a bit careless with matches perhaps." In his address, "The South and the New," he stirred the nation. He spoke of rebuilding Atlanta with "sunshine and love in every brick." It was the first time a Southern voice had spoken eloquently since the war. His message of love, peace, hope, and reconciliation came from a cleansed heart.

Few persons can retreat as did Grady, but most persons need a catharsis—a cleansing of heart—as he did. It is practical to take whatever steps and time necessary to achieve it. The peace and power resulting from the purity make it worth the price. The consequence makes it worth the cost in time and/or money.

The fountain must be pure if the stream is to flow with pure water. It will do no good to pave the creekbed if the springs of its source are contaminated. Room fresheners will be futile if the source of atmospheric pollution is not corrected. External reform does no lasting good if there is not an internal cleansing of the life. The pure heart is one free of pollutants such as greed, guile, and guilt. It can only be purged by divine means.

Reservoir

Huck Finn, the legendary character of Mark Twain's imagination, spoke the truth when he said, "Sometimes a fellow's conscience takes up more room than all the rest of a person's insides." The conscience of which he spoke is the counterpart of a contaminated heart.

The heart of which Christ spoke is not our physical organ. This rugged organ is a four-chambered, four-valved pump which handles 5,000 gallons of blood a day. That is almost enough to fill a railroad tank car. It supplies the circulatory system through 12,000 miles of vessels. In the course of a lifetime, it beats 2,500,000 times. Its function is vital to our physical life. In the spiritual realm Christ is the invisible heart.

He is no less vital to one's moral and spiritual life.

Heart is a synonym for the total person. It is the seat of personality. The entire inner life is referred to as the heart. To the Hebrew it included intellect (rational), emotions (aesthetic), volition (will).

Heart is prosaic language referring to the inner self. Jesus is spoken of as being the only person who ever lived life inside out.

In the New Testament era, medical science was still undeveloped. Common concepts held that the blood carried thought. When blood carrying a thought coursed through the brain, it became a conscious thought. The physical heart was known to pump blood. They concluded that all thought originated in the heart. Therefore, it was used descriptively to refer to all consciousness. It was a summary expression for the self.

My family and I motored leisurely down the mountains from Ridgecrest, North Carolina, toward Old Fort, few miles away. There we crossed a polluted stream. It was first called to our attention by the smell. It was so badly contaminated that it had developed a most unpleasant odor. Turning off the main road, we wound our way to the end of the asphalt by a brook flowing through a field. There we got out of the car and started the strenuous climb up to Catawaba Falls. The struggle to the summit was rewarded by an unforgettable sight. Mystically, water gushed from a crystal clear spring. It hastened to the rim of a waterfall. Plummeting over, it cascaded several feet into a chilly, clear pool. The water spray was caught by the sunlight and turned into a rainbow of color. The mist that filled the air refreshed our hot faces. These was even a sweetness to the atmosphere.

This captivating climate had to be left all too soon. Slowly and reluctantly, we began our descent. We passed a place where picnickers had thrown leftovers into the stream. A short distance further, an abandoned camp fire had been kicked into the water. Near the base was a mountaineer's cabin. They had been throwing their waste into the stream. As we got into our car and started home, we passed a mill that was belching its residue into the stream.

Suddenly it dawned on us that the dirty, stale stream we saw near the town had its source in the clear, clean waterfall at the summit. The further one got from the source, the greater the contamination.

It was in this same light that Jesus encouraged his followers to stay close to the source—to keep their hearts pure.

The significantly clear work *Peer Gynt* by Hendrik Ibsen speaks to the subject of the heart. In his latter years, this past master of self-seeking engaged in a rare moment of reflection. The worn-out wanderer began slowly to peel away the layers of an onion. His vivid imagination prompted him to consider each fold as representative of some experience of his past. Every strip moved him imaginatively into an epoch of bygone days. As he tossed away portions, he mused over such things as his shipwreck experience, valiant voyages, and heroic deeds. This one was Peer Gynt, the merchant; this Peer Gynt, the prophet. His multiple roles were recalled fondly.

As the peelings grew greater in number, he began to think what a large number of folds lie around the core of the onion. His active mind prompted him to question what he would find at the actual center. The core, he thought, will stand for Peer Gynt himself, the true man, his inner self. This was to be the true person apart from all the roles he had played and relationships he developed. What will be at the center? Impatience grew, and he began to strip away larger sections. At last he reached what should have been the core. He mused, "There is no kernel: It's all outsides!"

This poem looks into the heart of every person. Strip away all relationships and involvements. Remove all pretense and veneer. What is left at the center? It is in the heart, the real person, that purity is required.

The importance of this bastion of beliefs is illustrated in the lives of two knights of the Round Table.

It was impurity that barred the vision of Sir Lancelot and prevented him from seeing the Holy Grail. The fervently sought cup was thought to be the symbol and vehicle of the blood of Christ. All that was "pure, noble, and knightly" in him "twined and clung 'round that one sin, until the wholesome flower and poisonous grew together, each as each, not to be plucked asunder." Even when he came to Castle Carbonek, his ambition was unfulfilled. As he looked down the hall where the cup floated in luminous air, his vision was veiled. "A stormy glare, a heat as from a seven-times heated furnace, blasted and burnt and blinded him." The impurity in his life kept him from that which was most pure.

Tennyson's Galahad is made to say, "My strength is as the strength of ten, because my heart is pure." We respect Lancelot because of his bravery in battle. We admire Galahad because of his virtuous loyalty to his vow of knighthood. This purity he maintained even when in the home of another man's wife. Galahad was not just right; he was bright. Morals are not intended to make life harder, just happier. One of our nation's premier pioneers observed, "Sin is not hurtful because it is forbidden. Sin is forbidden because it is hurtful." That ageless couplet can save much grief if accepted.

The pure in heart choose, chart, and commit to their course. G. K. Chesterton said of Joan of Arc, "She chose her path and went down it like a thunderbolt." A pure heart produces tenacity of will. All resources are put at the disposal of a refined resolve.

Result

A person sees that for which he has eyes. Two persons can walk in the woods—one an unschooled person familiar with the outdoors, the other a botanist. The former sees trees and weeds. The botanist sees specimens and specific species of plants. Two persons may view the sky—one an uninformed city dweller who has never really seen the sky because of street lights, the other an astronomer. The astronomer sees and identifies glaxies, planets, and constellations. The other sees only "little twinklies."

The pure in heart see God. This is the bliss of those without mixed motives. What we know influences what we see. The light of understanding results from mental vision. The state of mind affects one's vision.

There is a strange linking in the Bible. Such impurities as adultery, fornication, lasciviousness, uncleanliness, and greed are associated with idolatry. One who commits idolatry has eyes for his god. These acts and emotions become gods themselves. They absorb the interest and demand the attention of their devotees. Such a state of life keeps one from seeing the true and living God. They are not looking in the right place or with the proper focus. Persons of such temperaments would not recognize him if they saw him. Often a complaint is raised by the idolater regarding not seeing God. It might be for the same reason that a bank robber doesn't see a policeman. They have different interests and are going different directions.

To see God means to know and experience him. It involves enjoying his presence and relationship.

To see God means to commune with him, to be refreshed by a love relationship with him, to be conscious of his omnipresence.

To see God means to behold him in everything. The Bible speaks of God as being in heaven. In doing so, it addresses the subject of his greatness, not his location. He is also here. He is a spirit and not to be viewed by the natural eye. Yet his handiwork is visible everywhere. The pure in heart see him in nature, health, pain, life, death, defeat, victory, weakness, and strength.

Upon entering an art gallery such as the Louvre, some see paintings. Artists see configurations, colors, combinations, and artistic genius. Upon entering the world, some see only created things. The pure in heart see the Creator of things.

To see means more than to behold or look at. It carries the idea of an interview or an audience. It is symbolic speech referring to intimate friendship. The Greeks who said, "Sir, we would see Jesus" were desirous of consulting with him.

Not everyone can see the head of state. There are requirements. Those who would commune with the Father must comply with his stipulations. Prayer is a form of spiritual consultation, an intimate fellowship. It is consultation at its best. Only the pure in heart can enjoy such an audience.

The crown of Eastern monarchs often rested uncertainly on insecure heads. There was a perpetual danger of some assassin trying to get to the king. Devious means were used to try to deceive his guards and gain access for personal gain as a threat to the king's life. No one could go in to see the king without his permission. Not even his queen could go into his chamber without his consent. Extensive efforts were made to secure the king's safety. Only one person had access to the king without first being invited. The prime minister could come and go at will. The prime minister was a friend chosen by the king because of his unswerving loyalty and unquestioned devotion. It was known that he always had the king's best interests at heart. His only reason for wanting to see the king was to serve him. Such a one was spoken of as having a pure heart. Theirs was a relationship of love. He could, therefore, commune with the king. He was conscious of his presence.

During the 1976 Democratic Presidential Nominating Convention in New York City, I went to the American Hotel to visit candidate Carter. His family was housed on the twenty-first floor. His working suite, where he was interviewing potential vice-presidential candidates, was also on that floor. Floors twenty and twenty-one were blocked off. For security reasons, no admission was allowed. I got off on the nineteenth floor amid a mass of reporters and interested spectators. Billy Carter met me there and escorted me through several security checkpoints. Rosalynn Carter met us on the twentieth floor. From there we walked through a number of other security stations. All totalled, we cleared fifteen different security checks. Not once did anyone inspect me. At some points Mrs. Carter blithely said, "Nelson is OK, but you might need to check Billy."

Once past the twentieth floor there was once again a calm,

quiet atmosphere. We moved down the colorfully carpeted corridor to the massive double doors leading into the presidential suite. Mrs. Carter graciously opened the door, and we walked right in. No one bothered to frisk us. The front-running nominee, Jimmy Carter, warmly greeted me with outstretched hands. A refreshing personal interchange followed.

My entrance into this intimate inner chamber was uncontested. I was known by the proper persons to be a well-intended friend. They knew that I had his interests at heart. My motive in coming was pure. During the convention, I visited that floor several times. Each time a family member escorted me, and there were no attempts to stop us. My attitude gave me access.

This Beatitude, like all the others, has a present and future fulfillment. The pure in heart shall someday enter into the presence of God's eternal heavenly home through the portal called death. They shall, in that moment, be more alive than ever.

To see means to know. We know about him now and imagine his greatness and glory. Ultimately, the pure in heart shall know him fully. "Every man that hath this hope in him, purifieth himself, even as he is pure" (1 John 3:3).

> This beatitude speaks of PURITY
>   meaning to be free of deception, defilement, and
>   division of loyalty.
> It talks of a PLACE,
>   the heart, meaning the intellect, emotions, and voli-
>   tion—
>   the total self.
> It refers to a PRIVILEGE,
>   seeing God, meaning to contemplate, communicate,
>   and
>   consult with God.
> The pure in heart shall ultimately see him
>   in his eternal holy of holies.

7
How to Find Your Roots

Peacemakers are happy people. When they bridge an estranged relationship, they bring together that which was not intended to be separated: Such action emulates Christ's character. His mission was reconciliation. He has passed that joyous role on to his followers. Persons who fulfill that responsibility evidence a characteristic of their happy elder brother, Jesus Christ. Happiness is a by-product of the process.

Robert Louis Stevenson wrote:

> In his own life, then, a man is not to expect happiness, only to profit by it gladly, when it shall arise; he is on duty here; he knows not how or why, and does not need to know; he knows not for what hire, and must not ask. Somehow or other, though he does not know what goodness is, he must try to be good; somehow or other, though he cannot tell what will do it, he must try to give happiness to others.

There is an air of despair and futility in that unguided attitude. His conclusion is correct, but unattainable with the attitude manifested. Happiness, as stated, should not be expected. It is always a bonus. The point missed is the duty assignment. We are sent to wage peace. The campaign, not its consequence, brings happiness.

Samuel Butler must have given great thought to the subject of happiness because he said: "Happiness and misery consist in a progression toward better or worse; it does not matter how high up or low down you are; it depends not on this, but on the direction in which you are tending." Those who tend to progress in peacemaking are sure to achieve happiness.

Happiness, a state of being perpetually sought after, is not an obtainable object in itself. It is a beautiful by-product of a worthy job well done. Peacemaking is a worthy job. The Chinese philosopher Chuang-tse spoke to this point: "Perfect happiness is the absence of the striving for happiness." Those who seek it as an end in itself, to be sought and/or bought, are the farthest from it.

Happiness has been a condition desired through the ages. A failure to realize the course by which to achieve it has caused more uhappiness. It compounds its misery. It is not embodied, as is so commonly thought, in people, places, or things. Actually, such can be a hindrance or a handicap to happiness.

Tolstoy observed, "Man is meant for happiness, and this happiness is in him." The happiest people are those who have the greatest capacity within themselves. Position and possession have nothing to contribute to happiness. Contrition and condition of the heart do.

Happiness is often spoken of as coming into one's life. Actually, it comes out of one's life. It cannot exude from a life that is engaged in counterproductive activities. When there are actions and attitudes contrary to happiness-producing character, it is impossible to be happy.

A mistake often made is to anticipate a state of euphoria at all times. No emotion can be maintained indefinitely. None! Anger, elation, sadness, grief, ecstasy, sorrow, bitterness, and even happiness as an emotion cannot be perpetually sustained. Emotions by their very nature must change. There can be a dominant one. Happiness is one of the most virtuous ones.

Seneca came close to reality when he noted, "Whatever is to make us better or happy, God has placed either openly before us or close to us." Actually, he has placed it within us. The realm of happiness is ruled over by principles. These are enunciated in the Beatitudes. Happiness is the harvest resulting from planting the right seed. Those who seek to achieve happiness on cheap terms get only a cheap thrill. Happiness can never be picked in the world's garden. He is happiest who best understands its source.

Dhammapada once wrote, "Full of love for all things in the world, practicing virtue, in order to benefit others, this man alone is happy." The virtue advocated in this seventh beautiful attitude is peacemaking.

Peacemaker (eirēnopoios), peace (eirēnē), to make (poieō) means the establishment of peace and concord. Those who disinterestedly come between contending parties and try to make peace are peacemakers. Peace is a harmonious relationship between parties resulting in a sense of rest and contentment. *Shalom,* the Hebrew equivalent, primarily signifies wholeness.

Devotees of the Prince of Peace have no room in their dispositions for argumentation, bigotry, contention, jealousy, quarrelsomeness, strife, and variance. For one to be a peacemaker, he must be at peace. The right relationship precedes the right result. Thomas à Kempis candidly commented, "First keep thy self in peace, and then thou shalt be able to keep peace among others." Personal peace is a subjective attitude resulting in objective action. It identifies one as a member of God's family. Possessors of peace are stable and adjusted. This peace is individual and internal.

Personal Peace

Every soul longs for peace as the ocean shell, when placed to the ear, seems to sigh for the untroubled depths of its native home. Peace is pictured in many ways. There is peace in the quiet calm waters of a mountain lake, sheltered from the winds by giant cliffs. There is peace in the eye of a hurricane that sweeps the land with its fury. There is peace in the silent blue depths of space. This hints that there is peace for humankind, whose nature is complex, composite, and compounded.

Personal peace is achieved by establishing a right relationship between the Creator and the creature. It has long been observed that he has made us for himself. We are never at peace until we are at peace with him. Heaven, through Christ, waged peace with humankind. Every imaginable initiative has been taken by God the Father to reach peace terms with persons.

Two primary obstacles to this existed. Man had breached God's holiness and justice. In the person of Christ, God settled those issues. The holy one died for unholy ones; the righteous one died for unrighteous ones; the just one died for unjust ones. Thus, the sin penalty was paid. All that remains is for the individual to accept the terms arranged. When this is done, the righteousness of Christ is imputed to the new believer. This transforms the life. The same ingredients are in the person's makeup. They are just transformed.

For Christmas one year, I secretly made a large ceramic elephant for my wife. Although it lacked a bit being life-sized, it was big enough to serve as an end table. After tooling it, the process of painting it began. The colors were drab and depressing—that combination would add no class to a room. After it had been painted, however, it was put in a kiln and fired. It remained in the large oven at a constant temperature of 1,983 degrees for over four hours. When the fire cooled and it was removed, it emerged as a new creation. The colors had been transformed. It was now orange, green, gold, and several other earth tones. Now, instead of being soft and fragile, it was solid and strong. Its nature had been changed. It was the same substance, but a new creation.

Personal peace is achieved through a similar spiritual process. The life that has had divided allegiance to a multiplicity of false gods becomes united within itself by devotion to one God. This is such a transition that Christ referred to it as being "born again." This new nature can enable one to accept self as the created object of a Creator who knows more and loves more fully than imagined. Once this peace is established, then one can engage in the process of trying to establish peace between parties.

Peace in Society

Peacemakers are bridge builders, fence menders, and reconcilers between parties. Peacemakers are not passive. They strive to bring estranged persons together.

Peacemakers are not meddlers. They have no selfish goals. Compassion for the welfare of others prompts aggressive love efforts at bringing parties together. Peacemakers are arbitrators. Every peacemaker is a fighter, but not every fighter is a peacemaker. Peacemakers fight in peace as well as for peace. They extend themselves on behalf of others, but are seldom self-protective.

Occasionally, this effort gets one in trouble. Remember, "The servant is not greater than his lord" (John 13:16). Peter declared, "Yet if any man suffer as a Christian, let him not be ashamed; but let him glorify God on this behalf" (1 Pet. 4:16). Rebuttals and rebuffs are sure to come; "He that was born after the flesh persecuteth him that was born after the Spirit" (Gal. 4:29). Followers of Christ can act knowing they may be "Persecuted, but not forsaken" (2 Cor. 4:9). The Prince of Peace warned, "If the world hate you, ye know that it hated me before it hated you" (John 15:18).

We, as he did, should pray, "Father, forgive them" (Luke 23:34). Keep right on publishing "glad tidings of peace." Our prototype said, "Let not your heart be troubled" (John 14:1).

Peacemakers can achieve great peace. There is an inherent reward in the effort, regardless of the effect.

Two familiar illustrations from the pages of literature demonstrate the advantages of peacemaking.

Robert Louis Stevenson told of two maiden sisters who lived in Edinburgh long ago. They shared a single room which was large, but it was still only one room. The two had a quarrel. Controversy divided them. Their bitterness was so deep that they never spoke a word to each other. Yet they still lived together. For whatever reason, they continued to keep house together. A chalk line drawn across the room separated the domains. Both the door and fireplace were bisected by it. Each could come and go and do her own cooking without violating the territory of the other. For years they co-existed in hostility. Even at night each could hear the breathing of her enemy. There was no reprieve. Never did four walls look upon uglier displays of unsisterliness. The closeness and coldness of the two estranged persons depicts conditions that prevail between many who need a peacemaker.

The Prince of Peace has difficulty demonstrating the benefits of peace where people are not peaceable. The reestablishment of proper relationships can result in spiritual revival.

In my hometown, two sisters refused to speak for years. A casual mistake in identity alienated the two. The caldron of their vituperation boiled over into the entire church. It was a house of hostility, not one of worship. So cold was the climate of assemblies that one would have had to use ice skates to profess Christ.

After years, by God's grace the two were reconciled. Theirs was great joy. As their bitterness had tainted the town, so their joy flooded it. Within days there was a great spiritual awakening in the church. Fellowship was renewed and happiness abounded. The work of a peacemaker had benefited many.

Oliver and Herbert Vivian tell a strange story of two nuns in their work *Romance of Religion*. As Bernardines, the nuns lived side by side in adjoining cells for five years. They ate at the same table and prayed in the same chapel. One of them died. According to the custom of the order, the dead nun was placed in the chapel with her face uncovered. The other nuns passed by. As her longtime next-door neighbor passed by and looked upon her face, she emitted a loud shriek and swooned. She had just recognized her dearest friend from whom she had parted in anger years before. Each had misunderstood the other and thought the other unaffected by the quarrel. For five years the two had lived side by side without even so much as hearing the voice of the other. Both would have done well to have copied the God they professed to follow.

"We are like islands," said Rudyard Kipling, "and we shout to each other across seas of misunderstanding. Like ancient Athens, Queen of the Sea, we need to send out our ships to all regions. The vessels of peace sail well. It is an heavenly breeze that propels them."

Some years ago the Calvary Baptist Church in downtown Washington, D.C., received three gifts in perpetuity—an organ, a bell, and a clock. A former pastor spoke of the symbolism of the three gifts.

"The organ reminds us that we need harmony in the world and in our hearts.

"The bell reminds us that we need to call the world back to God, if the world is to have harmony.

"The clock reminds us that we do not have forever to get on with the job."

In situations poisoned by injury and aggravated by evasion of responsibility, the peacemaker is needed. An atmosphere charged with recrimination can spontaneously erupt into violence. This is true of incidents on school buses, tenant stairways, athletic fields, diplomatic sessions, and halls of justice. Violence is never cathartic. It is always forgiveness that cleans and clears the air. This fact must be taken out of church wrappings and put into everyday practice.

The peacemaker uses such weapons as a spirit of goodwill, the ability to apologize, a smile, a request for pardon, and a congenial nature. Peacemaking is practical, daily work. Christ's admonition to do it was not intended as religious rhetoric. It was meant to be the daily calling of all of his followers. Christ left his followers a legacy of peace. Those who have been forgiven have most readily been given the capacity to forgive.

More wisely than Kipling, John Donne, nearly three hundred years ago, wrote in his "Devotions":

> No man is an island, entire of itself. Everyman is a piece of the continent, a part of the main; if a clod be washed away by the sea, Europe is less . . . any man's death diminishes me, because I am involved in mankind; and therefore never send to know for whom the bell tolls; it tolls for thee.

The peacemaker is "involved in mankind." Christ, whom we Christians call Lord, spoke compelling words regarding involvement. His encouragement to love our neighbor forbids us to remain detached.

The New Testament author, James, scoffed at the piousness of persons who say sweet things to people in trouble and don't lift a finger to help them. A central theme in the writings of James is that those who mean business for God get involved. There is no excuse for standing aloof. He even said that if we don't get involved, we are guilty of sin.

Peacemakers are not papier-maché people. They have heart. Because they do they act. They act lovingly even toward those who despise and ostracize them.

The celebrated poet Edwin Markham was once asked what he considered his greatest poem. One might think it "Lincoln," or "The Man with the Hoe." Without a moment's hesitation he said, "I wrote four lines which I treasure more than all else I wrote during my entire life." He then slowly repeated them:

> He drew a circle that shut me out—
> Heretic, rebel, a thing of flout.
> But love and I had a wit to win:
> We drew a circle that took him in.

That is the spirit of the peacemaker.

Martin Luther often told the story of two goats who met on a narrow bridge over deep water. "They could not go back; they durst not fight. After a short parley, one of them lay down and let the other go over him, and thus no harm was done. The moral," he would say, "is easy: Be content if thy person be trod upon for peace's sake. Thy person, I say, not thy conscience." That is a point that distinguishes a peacemaker. He is more concerned about principle than about his own person.

The peacemaker is thoughtful and tactful. The Chinese have a proverb that states: "If you talk with a soft voice, you do not need a thick stick." This proverb illumines the path to peace. Solomon wisely phrased it: "A soft answer turneth away wrath" (Prov. 15:1). This is the best expression of the manly art of self-defense. Kind speech defuses explosive situations.

Peacemakers are considerate of the reputation of others. "Mama, dear, I was a peacemaker today," said an excited child as she settled in her mother's lap. "How was that?" asked the mother. "I heard something, and I didn't tell it," was the reply. Peacemakers only tell the truth when love motivates them to speak. A confidence can be guarded by the peacemaker. The intent and desire is to protect the well-being of others. Backbiting, belittling, gossiping, murmuring, and sowing of seeds of discontent are not in the character of the peacemaker. He will not hear or repeat any account, the source of which cannot be identified as the point of truth.

There is an ancient Chinese proverb that corroborates the essence of this Beatitude.

> If there is righteousness in the heart, there will be beauty
> in the character. If there is beauty in the character, there
> will be harmony in the home. If there be harmony in the
> home, there will be order in the nation. When there is order
> in the nation, there will be peace in the world.

Peace with God

The ministry of the peacemaker fulfills its loftiest role when it establishes peace between a person and God. The highest good for any life is this. It is so because of the lasting result. It has an eternal consequence. No joy can compare with the thrill of making such an introduction. In helping to establish a right relationship between a person and God, peace with an eternal dimension is established. There is pleasure in seeing a young child with an unspoiled life come to him. There is no less delight in seeing the hardened belligerent repentantly come to his terms.

This is the primary reason the Father leaves his children in this pilgrim land without taking them home immediately. The Son of man came to seek and to save. He said he had to be about his Father's business. That business was to bring people to know the peace only he can give.

Peace begins with a cleansing process. Forgiveness must be obtained before peace can be maintained.

The Goths were led on a wide-ranging conquest by Alaric I. His rugged hosts poured over the walls of Rome which sprawled before him. He subdued the luxurious land of Italy as far south as Sicily. At Cosenza in Calabria he became ill and died. His followers were faced with a dilemma. What could they do with the body of their dead leader? It was impossible to carry it across the great plains of Italy and over the Alps to the dark forest of his fatherland. If it were publicly buried, it would later be desecrated. They elected to divert the course of the River Busento and bury him in the river channel. Once finished, the river grave was covered by the waters as they flowed again in their natural basin.

The Goths had given their leader a grave which no hand could reach. It is such a grave as this which the heavenly Father prepares to cover sins of all who commit to him. His cleansing is so thorough that there is no trace of sins which have been forgiven. Once this guilt factor is removed, harmony can prevail. Thus, peace is possible. Peacemakers are dedicated to letting this good news be known.

The need for this peace is apparent. Books on the subject sell well. Drugs that anesthetize and stupefy, thus producing false peace, abound. As long as material goods abound, their possessors are sometimes insulated and do not feel an immediate need for peace. Many persons are like the character in *The History of Mr. Polly* of whom H. G. Wells said, "He was not so much a person as a civil war." One young man said, "I made myself god, and my god let me down." A blithe, middle-aged woman declared, "I feel like a committee that is constantly quarreling."

When given an opportunity to share Christ, the peacemaker should rejoice. It is an occasion to help persons who share the frustrations like those expressed. There should be no timidity about offering a person the greatest gift possible.

A peacemaker has to earn the right to be an arbitrator of the Almighty. This is done by living a life in character with the nature of Christ. Those who claim to be Christians, Christ-partisans, must practice what they preach before they can preach. The life and the lips must be in concert.

God's Forever Family

Peacemakers shall be called God's children. "Shall be called" is a Hebrew expression meaning "shall be acknowledged to be."

A group of Swiss researchers have done an extensive, intriguing study. They have compared photographs of husbands and wives who have lived together more than ten years. The analysis showed that these persons had actually grown to look more alike than either did their parents. Close association had even affected their appearance.

Spiritually, this principle is applicable. Peacemakers who live close to their heavenly Father soon begin to resemble him. This prompts persons to acknowledge them as children of God. They resemble the root of their being.

There is dignity in the title "children of God." It is an expression meaning "to partake of the nature of." Those who partake of his nature are peacemakers acknowledged to be his children.

Our Elder Brother has left us the legacy of peacemaking.

PEACEMAKERS are partakers,
    remakers, and barrier breakers.
The prototype Peacemaker is
    the Prince of Peace.
He waged peace.
    He died trying.
Peacemakers are aggressors,
    but not all aggressors are peacemakers.
Peacemakers are expendable,
    but peace is indispensable.
There is no peace without a peacemaker.

It does not emerge, evolve, or egress
    from an ethereal state of nothingness.
Peace must be made by peacemakers.
This act so resembles the attitude and action
    of our heavenly Father
that those who wage peace
    are called progeny of the Prince of Peace.

8
How to Grin and Bear It

"Happiness is as a butterfly, which, when pursued, is always beyond our grasp, but which, if you will sit down quietly, may alight upon you," wrote Nathaniel Hawthorne.

Peace amid persecution sounds paradoxical. Everything about these seaside statements sounds like inverted speech. How can a butterfly light in a storm? That is just the point; it has to light during a storm. It does where there is solitude. Likewise, happiness even amid tribulation perches where there is a controlled haven. The heart is this cove apart.

El Yunque, *the anvil,* is a mammoth mountain that rises into the clouds along the coast of Puerto Rico. It forms a barrier against which clouds blowing in from the sea build up. As a result, it rains several times a day on the upper elevations. A lush rain forest has developed. A climb there is a treat for the senses. Lovely tropical vegetation shades the trial. Brilliant flowers bloom throughout. Ferns grow to a height of forty feet. One of the most interesting inhabitants of the region is a tiny green frog known as Coquí. He is distinct from other frogs in that instead of croaking, he whistles. During a rain, the area is alive with his sharp sounds. Inexplicably, if one is taken to any other part of the world, he never again whistles. Once removed from his element, he becomes mute.

Happiness is much the same. It thrives in a certain environment. If removed, it withers. In the Beatitudes, Christ outlined the natural habitat in which happiness thrives. If these conditions prevail in the heart, happiness prevails. Externals cannot retard it. Like the Coquí who sings best in the rainstorms, happiness is even more distinct amid persecution.

If we would only observe, we would see that happy people are doers. The more noble the cause, the greater the happiness. If looking for a happy person, you will find him busy: building a doghouse, writing a book, educating his child, growing African violets, or digging for dinosaur eggs in the Gobi Desert. He will not be searching for happiness as if it were a contact lens lost in shag carpet. He never probes for it as an end in itself. Those who have it suddenly become aware that they are happy in the course of pursuing a worthy goal.

Horace Bushnell observed, "Life is always dull and insipid to those who have no great works on their hands to do and no lofty ideals to elevate their spirits." A big cause makes a person big. One takes on the size and stature of the goals and responsibilities that consume him.

A person with a cause so dear to him that he will endure persecution for it has found a lofty one. One so self-consuming has the potential of great happiness. The annals of martyrdom are filled with accounts of saints expressing their joy in death. Such persons have not lived with a ghoulish, insatiable appetite for death. A martyr complex has not maddened them. They are merely consumed with a cause. Death is not considered too great a price to pay for it.

"The greatest use of time," noted William James, "is to spend it for something that outlasts it." Self-preservation is often a synonym for selfishness. It can be a cop-out because of a lack of conviction. It can produce guilt, but never long-lasting happiness—regrets, but not rejoicing.

Persecuted (diōkō) means put to flight, driven away and pursued. The apostle Paul spoke of the living enactment of this Beatitude in 2 Corinthians 4:

	Troubled on every side, yet not in distress.
	Handicapped,
TRIBULATION:	but never frustrated.
	Sore pressed at every point,
	but never hemmed in.

Perplexed,
   but not in despair.
Puzzled,
CONSTERNATION: but never forlorn.
At wit's end,
   but never at hope's end.
Persecuted,
   but not forsaken.
Harassed,
ISOLATION: but never standing alone.
Plagued,
   but never abandoned by God.
Cast down,
   but not destroyed.
Knocked down,
CONFRONTATION: but never knocked out.
Off our feet,
   but never unconscious.

Don't Shun It

In Matthew 5:1–10, Jesus had used a word translated *they*. Starting in verse 11, he used the word *ye*. Thus, he implied that his followers in every generation may suffer persecution; but in verse 11, he indicated that those who comprised his first audience would suffer persecution. Christ prophesied, and tradition confirms that only one of the twelve died peaceably.

Persecution became so heavy that by the end of the first century the word for *witness* and the one for *martyr* became the same.

Proper persecution became both a birthmark and a landmark for Christ's early followers. A Spirit-filled worker connected with the African Inland Mission told a story which portrays this principle. He said that he was often instructed on how to get to a certain point by being warned of various dangers. Instructions might relate to a dangerous river crossing, a wooded area inhabited by wild animals, or a snake-infested marsh. When he would come to one of these areas, he would know that he was on the right path. The hazards actually helped to identify his progress. Our Lord told his followers that righteousness often resulted in tribulation. Rather than being resented, it should be accepted as an encouragement, identifying the path Christ proposed.

No follower of Christ should ever fear the frown of the world. If a blind man bumps into you, you don't resent him. Most persons would feel compassion for the man. There would be no real shock at its happening. Likewise, when the world responds with persecution, that should not be shocking. Both acts are in character. Each is acting within his capacity.

Strange as it may seem, it has been persecution that has brought many to Christ.

Adoniram Judson suffered great agony in stocks while in a prison in Burma. Upon being released, he asked the king's permission to go to a specified city to preach. "I am willing for a dozen preachers to go to that city," replied the king, "but not you. Not with those hands. My people are not fools enough to listen to and follow your words, but they will not be able to resist those scarred hands." He, as the apostle Paul, bore in his body the marks of Jesus Christ. His scarred hands were authoritative.

Historians record that many gladiators in the Roman arenas were brought to faith in Christ by the facial expressions of believers faced with death. Their bearing and demeanor was such as to attest of Christ's presence. The persecuted paved the path to the kingdom of heaven for many.

A little clipping that crossed my desk depicts how persecution can be productive.

> Life on earth would not be worth much if every source of irritation were removed. Yet most of us rebel against the things that irritate us, and count as heavy loss what ought to be rich gain. We are told that the oyster is wiser; that when an irritating object, like a bit of sand, gets under the "mantle" of his shell, he simply covers it with the most precious part of his being and makes a pearl out of it. The

irritation that it was causing is stopped by encrusting it with the pearly formation. A true pearl is therefore simply a VICTORY over irritation. Every irritation that gets into our lives today is an opportunity for pearl culture. The more irritations the devil flings at us, the more pearls we may have. We need only to welcome them and cover them completely with love, that most precious part of us, and the irritation will be smothered out as the pearl comes into being. What a store of pearls we may have, if we will!

The early church recognized and responded to persecution as a means by which Christ could be glorified. It was an opportunity more than an offense.

Death is the ultimate end of persecution. Even it is but a passage. John Bunyan's character, Faithful, is depicted at the stake in *The Pilgrim's Progress* in the following manner.

Now I saw that there stood behind the multitude a chariot and a couple of horses waiting for Faithful, who (so soon as his adversaries had dispatched him) was taken up into it and straightway was carried up through the clouds with sound of a trumpet, the nearest way to the celestial gate.

Death to the believer is but a means to an end. Even the ultimate form of persecution has a purpose.

In the Yellowstone Park area of America grows an unusual evergreen, the lodgepole pine. Like other pines, its cones must stay on the tree for years. Even when they fall off, they usually do not open. They open only when exposed to extreme heat. Forest fires frequently destroy great expanses of this beautiful country. At the same time the heat opens the cones of the lodgepole pine. They are often the first tree to grow in a fire-ravaged area. The seed of new life is waiting for the right conditions.

Similarly, the church owes Paul to the seed of Stephen's blood. The name of those comparably won is Legion, for they are many. It is impossible to count the apples in a seed. Only heaven knows the number of converts resulting from observing faithful response by those persecuted.

Perhaps there has been no century in which more Christians

have suffered greater persecution than the twentieth century. On every continent the tales of atrocities performed on believers are frightening. Literally millions in Europe, Africa, Asia, and South America died for their faith. Organized efforts at eradicating followers of Christ have been made in several countries. Even in China, where the bloodiest purges occurred, the underground church flourishes. A resurgence of belief in Russia has occurred. Several Russian space scientists have privately spoken to American space technicians about their faith, which has been fueled by scientific evidences of a Creator-Designer. Purges often tend to purify and propagate the faith. It is a story of survival of the spiritual fittest.

Persecution hides its hideous face behind many different masks in America. Ostracism, hostility, rejection, insult, and mockery are ways in which it masquerades. Instinctively, everyone desires social acceptance. Often the righteous suffer rejection, falsehood, and witty harassment. Such wounds, though not often fatal, are painful. Though mild in manner, they are injurious in effect. A promotion passed over, an invitation not extended, a dinner denied, a position on the club not granted, or a friendly informal gathering from which one is excluded can be persecution. Actually, these are ways in which the world tells the Christians they just don't belong in this setting. The Christian should have already figured that out for himself and not feel hurt.

Don't Seek It

Not everyone with the look of a martyr on his face will wear a martyr's crown on his head. Self-made martyrs are egotists with a sick sense of virtue. Some personalities fish for persecution like a fisherman does a large fish. They do everything they can to snag people. They are persecuted because of their tactlessness and temperament and boast as though it were for righteousness. Thus, they get a spiritual ego trip. These are nothing but antagonists who will not allow people to leave them alone. They are resented and rebuffed, not for the sake of the Kingdom, but because they are simply impossible to live with. This is their way of searching for identity.

Our breakfast table overlooks a shaded deck. Beautiful trees grow close to the house. The angle of the sun's rays on the window often results in a mirror effect. Those on the outside can't see in; they can only see their own image reflected. One morning I sat at the table and watched a frustrated bird fight with its mirror image in the windowpane. Finally, in exhaustion, he turned from his struggle and in defeat flew away. He had no cause for a fight. He had no enemy. He was his own worst enemy. Many persons consider themselves persecuted, while in reality they are just flattering themselves by picking on themselves. If you are going to get in a struggle, make sure it is a worthy one.

Any Christian who is persecuted has only one valid reason for it—he is like Jesus Christ. That is what being righteous, practicing righteousness, really is. Jesus stated it simply: "If the world hate you, ye know that it hated me before it hated you. If ye were of the world, the world would love his own: but because ye are not of the world, but I have chosen you out of the world, therefore, the world hateth you. Remember the word that I said unto you, The servant is not greater than his lord. If they have persecuted me, they will also persecute you" (John 15:18–20).

There is no other legitimate reason for a believer to be persecuted. All other reasons might well be because of personality quirks or character flaws, but not righteousness.

This passage does not say:

"Blessed are the objectionable . . ." There is no virtue in simply protesting every move others make. This is often done simply because the person is not liked, not because what he is doing is unrighteous. Competitiveness can contribute to this cutting conduct.

"Blessed are the obstinate . . ." There is no value in being hardheaded. This is often one's nature, but never a part of the new nature. Some individuals who are prone to protest about everything try to cover it under the guise of righteousness. Simple congeniality and basic courtesy can compensate for this character corrosion.

"Blessed are the offensive . . ." There is no valid reason to add offended persons to a collection, much as one does charms for a bracelet. Some headhunters think this is an evidence of their Christian commitment. In reality it is a revelation of their carnal conduct. Few persons are attracted to Christ by people who repel them.

"Blessed are the ostentatious . . ." There is no victory in that which is demonstrative and not developmental. A pious show of superficial statements and acts has no productive purpose. Some individuals make a show even by their inflection in pronouncing their "A-M-E-N" to inspiring statements. Religious gobbledygook and garb are garbage.

"Blessed are the oppressive . . ." There is no vitality in being unjustly harsh. External codes of conduct created to suit someone's personal taste are improper reasons for crowing when persecuted. A tyrant clothed in modest apparel and quoting Scripture is no friend of the Kingdom. Such are Satan's decoys. They form insulation between a loving Lord and a lost world.

"Blessed are the overbearing . . ." There is no verdict of acquittal due the ungodly and lordly. Imperious personalities are sometimes excused as having strong convictions, when in reality they are simply dictatorial. The brazen, brash, brassy busybodies who seek to overpower people with their wisdom or personality are most often rejected as being repulsive rather than refreshing.

Don't seek persecution. It has a way of searching out the righteous without their quest for it. Some feel guilty if they are free of it for a time.

A number of years ago, Japan conquered Korea. Many leading Christians suffered extreme persecution. A number were tortured in Japanese jails. Others who were not persecuted felt that they were lacking something. A native pastor is reported to have asked a missionary, "Maksa, there must be something wrong with us Methodists. I fear that we are not living as godly as we ought to live. There are thirty-seven Presbyterians in jail and only one Methodist! Does not the Lord count us worthy to suffer shame for his name?"

If spared persecution, the Christian should rejoice. It may be a time in his life when he is receiving mercy or being comforted. Rejoice over peace; don't search for persecution.

Persecution can best be endured in light of its duration. At best, when compared to eternal life, it is brief.

One of the most fascinating ornate buildings I have ever seen is the Cathedral of Milan. It is worth the struggle required to get through the clouds of pigeons filling the square in front just to read the inscriptions over the triple doorways. Over one is carved a beautiful wreath of roses and beneath them the inscription: "All that which pleases is but for a moment." Over another is sculptured a cross with the words, "All that which troubles is but for a moment." Over the large central entrance is the statement, "That only is important which is eternal." Such a balanced perspective must be maintained at all times. Persecution passes.

While traveling through the beautiful mountains of North Carolina, my family and I were startled by the violence of a sudden storm. Its fury was so intense that it seemed intent on blowing away even the ageless mountains. The sky grew black. Raging winds rocked our car. The tempestuous rain was so heavy that it blinded our vision. We were forced to stop and wait for it to stop. It soon passed. Almost immediately the sun broke through. There in their ageless majesty stood the rain-refreshed mountains. The greenery blanketing their sides glistened in the sun. The storm had passed. Its spent fury purified the atmosphere and washed the countryside. Likewise, persecution purges.

It seems paradoxical that man's persecution and Christ's promises should converge on the same person. It is to those that the kingdom of heaven is promised.

One has noted, "The way to heaven is through heaven, and all the way to heaven is heaven, and only the heavenly enter heaven."

Heaven was what Christ had in mind when he said, "Great is your reward" (Matt. 5:12).

The Kingdom of Heaven

Jesus Christ said of those persecuted for righteousness' sake that "theirs is the kingdom of heaven" (Matt. 5:10). This expression is used thirty-three times in Matthew, but nowhere else in the Bible. Jesus himself used it twenty-nine of the times.

The kingdom of heaven is constituted of those who are poor in spirit, born of the spirit, have the Spirit of Christ, and who worship God in spirit and in truth.

These are all heavenly attitudes held by people on earth. Thus, the Kingdom begins here and now.

It is a community in which Christ reigns. Government involves voluntary obedience to him. There are no conscripts, and there is no constraint. As a natural consequence, the citizens are bound to each other by their mutual love for Christ.

A portion of Christ's model prayer helps to interpret the nature of the kingdom. He prayed, "Thy kingdom come. Thy will be done in earth, as it is in heaven" (Matt. 6:10). The first of these petitions is explained by the latter. Herein it is strongly suggested that where his will is done, his kingdom has come. His will is done perfectly in heaven. When it is done on earth, that extends the confines of the kingdom to that territory, also.

In this kingdom, Christ is Sovereign, Monarch, Master, Lord, Majesty, and King. In a more secular sense, he is: chairman of the board, president, director, and coach. He owns the controlling stock. In his domain, he is the unrivaled authority.

His followers do not possess the kingdom because they endure suffering. They endure suffering because they are possessed of the kingdom.

The kingdom of heaven is not so much a region as a reign. It refers basically to the rule of Christ in the life. It produces happiness because events are understood from the Lord's perspective. This rule prevails wherever one might be and under whatever conditions. It is not merely a reference to "pie in the sky by and by." However, the reign reaches its zenith in the eternal realm called heaven.

One does not attempt to enact the Beatitudes just to get to go to heaven. Because one is going to heaven, there is a strong desire to enact the Beatitudes. No synthetic spirit and forced labor can garner the glory of the gates of glory.

Illustrative of this was a delightful visit I was privileged to have to the White House. President and Mrs. Carter were kind enough to allow me to stay in the Lincoln Bedroom. This spacious room was where Mr. Lincoln signed the Emancipation Proclamation. A handwritten copy of his Gettysburg Address is on the desk. It is located on the floor with the presidential living quarters.

Immediately across the hall is the beautiful Queen's Bedroom. Its principal occupants have been heads of state. Late one evening, long after normal bedtime hours, I strolled back into this august room to look at the book I had seen there earlier. It was now well after midnight. The First Family had retired. The entire floor was otherwise vacant. Even the quiet of the evening was inspirational as I sat reading. Suddenly, my reverie was disrupted by the rapid patter of little feet. Hastily, I looked around just in time to see a dark streak dart across the corner of the room. The object moved in one door and out a nearby door so fast I could not identify it.

The next morning at the breakfast table I could contain my curiosity no longer. After explaining the experience, I noticed wry smiles all around the table. Then I asked, "Was that . . .? Could that have been . . .?"

"Yes," came the reply, "that was J. B."

J. B.? Why, I remembered J. B. from Plains, Georgia. One day J. B. showed up at Billy Carter's service station. He was so skinny and hungry that he looked weak. He had been abused so often that if you tried to stroke him, he would lie down and roll over. J. B. was just a stray little jet black mutt. He had no pedigree or other claim to fame. How, then, did J. B. get to the White House?

One day someone with authority and ability said, in effect, "J. B., I love you. Come on and go to the White House with me." Without protest J. B. responded in love and was carried along. Today the White House is J. B.'s pad. He has the run of the family living quarters. He is wanted and welcomed. He did not get there because he earned it, merited it, or deserved it. He got there because someone loved him enough to provide for him.

No person can ever do enough to earn the right to go to heaven. Provisions have been made for us. All we have to do is respond in love. This loving response results in Beatitudelike conduct while in transit.

> It is the cause of persecution,
>   not the case of persecution,
>   that counts.
> Persecution is not a virtue to be sought.
> Persecution is not a vice to be fought.
> Persecution must be interpreted as it ought.
> It can purge, purify, and prepare us.
> It can develop, discipline, and disciple.
> It can motivate, stimulate, and activate.
> At its worst it can do the best
>   by opening the gates of glory
>   for ultimate admission into the region
>   where Jesus reigns.
> Seek ye first the Kingdom!
>   If persecution results
> It is an indication that you are on your way,
>   not in his way.
> Heaven is worth the trip
>   even if you have to go through hell
>   to get there.